LEFT OF MATTHEW

:: NORMAN HUBBARD

LEFT OF MATTHEW

EXPLORING THE GREAT IDEAS OF THE OLD TESTAMENT ::

Our Guarantee to You

The Navigators is an international Christian organization. Our mission is to advance the gospel of Jesus and His kingdom into the nations through spiritual generations of laborers living and discipling among the lost. We see a vital movement of the gospel, fueled by prevailing prayer, flowing freely through relational networks and out into the nations where workers for the kingdom are next door to everywhere.

NavPress is the publishing ministry of The Navigators. The mission of NavPress is to reach, disciple, and equip people to know Christ and make Him known by publishing life-related materials that are biblically rooted and culturally relevant. Our vision is to stimulate spiritual transformation through every product we publish.

ISBN-10: 1-60006-052-8
ISBN-13: 978-1-60006-052-6

Cover design by studiogearbox.com
Cover image by Sergio Pitamitz/Robert Harding World Imagery
Creative Team: Nicci Hubert, Keith Wall, Debbie Weaver, Darla Hightower, Arvid Wallen, Pat Reinheimer

Printed in the United States of America

1 2 3 4 5 6 7 8 / 11 10 09 08 07

To the students and staff of
The Navigators campus ministry
at The University of Wisconsin-Eau Claire
from 1999–2006.
And especially to Joe and Ronni Bernardy,
who gave me the freedom to try many things
and fail at most of them.

"You shall therefore lay up these words of mine

in your heart and in your soul."

Deuteronomy 11:18, ESV

CONTENTS

INTRODUCTION 9
The Journey Ahead

1. OUR PLACE IN SPACE 13
Creation Sets the Story of Humanity in Motion

2. THE GRAVITY OF OUR FALL 27
Humanity's Plummet from Perfection to Imperfection

3. ONE FAMILY FOR ALL NATIONS 41
God's Chosen People Open a New Chapter in History

4. SHATTERING THE YOKE OF SLAVERY 55
Divine Deliverance from the Severest Trials

5. RIGHTEOUSNESS MADE PLAIN 71
The Law Enlightens Our Path Toward Liberty

6. GOD'S DWELLING AMONG HIS PEOPLE 85
Accommodations Fit for a King

7. A SUFFERING SOVEREIGN 99
Anticipating the Messiah's Appearance

8. ANTICIPATING THE DAWN 111
The Promise of a New Covenant and a New Era

9. JUDGMENT JUST OVER THE HORIZON 125
All Things Must Come to an End—Eventually

NOTES 139

ABOUT THE AUTHOR 143

INTRODUCTION

THE JOURNEY AHEAD ::

Christians worship God as Creator, Judge, Redeemer, and Friend. But seldom do we think of Him as an Author. It's time for us to expand our appreciation of the divine genius!

God penned sixty-six books. Why should any of us limit ourselves to studying only twenty-seven of them? God's works span three thousand years of human history. Why only read about the last sixty? But that's exactly what we do if we overlook the Old Testament.

If we closely follow Jesus' teaching, we would be hard-pressed to justify any apathy toward the Old Testament. When Jesus taught, He quoted the Old Testament, argued from it, and directed His disciples to think about it. If we intend to follow Jesus, He will lead us into an understanding of the entire Bible.

The study you hold in your hands will help you start this very journey.

No doubt, the Old Testament is thick. If you pinch the pages of your Bible together and compare the ones to the left of Matthew with the ones to the right of Malachi, you'll get an idea of just how much revelation awaits you in the Old Testament. But how much of the Old Testament have you actually read? How solid is your grasp of the great ideas presented in its pages? For many Christians, the Old Testament is a vast, under-explored collection of inspired writings taken to be authoritative yet imposing.

Consider how vast the Old Testament is. If you set out to read the whole Bible in a year, starting with Genesis on January 1 and ending with the maps in the back, you wouldn't reach the New Testament until mid-October! That's more than ten months of reading in the Old Testament before you ever read the first reference to Jesus in the gospel of Matthew.

When, if ever, have you spent ten months reading the Old Testament? What would happen if you did? How would you even begin?

On this unfamiliar continent, you could cross borders without even knowing it and meet people you don't remotely understand. Couldn't you just play it safe and stick to the familiar terrain of the New Testament, peppering your reading plan with a psalm here and a proverb there?

You could certainly try, but what will you do with the hundreds of allusions to the Old Testament throughout the New Testament? We can't even read the twenty-five verses in Jude without bumping into eight specific Old Testament references. How much less so the pivotal letters of Romans and Hebrews or the teachings of Jesus.

Of course, no sincere Christian really wants to avoid the Old Testament altogether. Most of us just want to avoid confusion, and the Old Testament can be confusing. I am reminded of the time my wife questioned our then five-year-old daughter about her Sunday school lesson.

"Were you studying about Elijah?" my wife asked.

"Yeah," our daughter answered, staring thoughtfully into space. "And Goliath and King Darius."

Either my daughter's kindergarten class had embarked on a comprehensive survey of the Old Testament from the united monarchy under

Saul to the Exile—or she was somewhat confused. All the names, dates, events, and people were tumbled together into one muddled collage.

Her experience is not unlike ours. The Old Testament can be confusing if you've never spent much time studying it. How could hundreds of pages of poetry, prophecy, proverbs, and narrative spanning three millennia prove otherwise when you first begin?

Yet too many of us end where we begin, leaving the Old Testament just the way we found it—a collection of extraordinary scenes and storybook morals, kind of like a baptized version of Aesop's fables. We develop a passing familiarity with Old Testament stories but reserve our serious religious reflection for the New Testament.

It's time to invest adult reflection, historical imagination, and theological substance into our reading of the Old Testament. It's time to rescue Elijah from Goliath (or was it King Darius?) and begin treating the Old Testament as divine revelation, not a helpful storybook or source for ancient quotations. It's time to take a guided tour through the Old Testament.

What you hold in your hands is a roadmap to help you on your journey. As with any map, this one is intended to chart a course through the great themes and big ideas of the Old Testament. But like any other map, this one can only take you so far: It can help you chart a course, but it can't make you move. It can offer a sensible route, but it can't ensure you will go the distance. More than all this, it cannot satisfy your deep longings to know God, any more than a map of Colorado could satisfy your desire to experience the Rocky Mountains by driving into the clouds on a narrow mountain pass.

You have to go there to experience it. You have to make the journey to live the reality. If it is deeper knowledge of God that you seek, you'll find it to the "left of Matthew." Enjoy the journey!

::1

OUR PLACE IN SPACE

CREATION SETS THE STORY OF HUMANITY IN MOTION ::

Nearly every person in the Western world grew up hearing the story of how God created the heavens and the earth, how Adam and Eve lived in the Garden of Eden, and how the snake tempted the first couple into making a really lousy decision. Even those brought up in families that weren't particularly religious may still have heard stories or read books about the Bible's version of the beginning of time.

In fact, the account of Creation in Genesis 1–2 is probably one of the best-known stories in the Bible. While it's wonderful that so many are acquainted with the creation story, this familiarity causes many people to gloss over the events and breeze over the details. Being accustomed to the broad strokes of the narrative may account for its relative *unimportance* in the lives of many believers. As G. K. Chesterton said, "It is almost impossible to make the facts vivid, because the facts are familiar; and for fallen men . . . familiarity is fatigue."[1] That's certainly true in regard to the creation story.

Let's set aside our familiarity and shake off the fatigue. Let's come at the story with an open mind and a fresh set of eyes. It will require some effort on your part, not just to read and write your way into an original investigation, but also to think historically and imaginatively about a story you could easily paraphrase.

As you prepare to come at the creation story as if for the first time, bear in mind the following: While the account of Creation is not incompatible with science, you won't be reading an ancient lab report. The Genesis narrative was not intended to be a scientific dissertation or a forensic investigation into the origins of humankind. And while the opening pages of Genesis describe our *prehistoric* origins, the work is self-evidently a *historic* production for a particular people, namely, the children of Israel. Genesis was written by a person and for a people who already believed in the God who said, "Let there be light." These people already addressed Him by the names *Elohim* and *Yahweh*—sacred and holy names for the One they knew to be their Creator. And they already believed themselves to be a chosen nation, under God.

What purpose, then, did the account of Creation serve in this community? Was it a concise retelling of explanations long offered about where everything had come from? Or was it just a sensible way to begin an account of the nation's formative years and founding figures? Could it have been written to promote fervent worship of the true God in religious gatherings? Or to make the standard of truth explicit against false teachings that were creeping into the community?

Keep all of these ideas in mind as you study the creation account in Genesis 1 and 2. Read the text with your powers of observation sharpened. Keep your mind open. Keep your heart open. For that matter, keep your eyes open so you can periodically gaze out your window into the sky. See if you do not agree with the brilliant scientist and theologian Blaise Pascal, who said the universe is so great a "sensible mark of the almighty power of God that imagination loses itself in the thought."[2]

THE OPEN ROAD

Read Genesis 1–2.

::CREATED TO MAKE

Two distinct words are used of God's creative power in Genesis 1 and 2. The word *created* (*bara'* in Hebrew) in Genesis 1:1 signifies that God brought the material world into existence *from nothing*. The word *made* (*'asah*) in Genesis 1:7 and following passages signifies that God fashioned the matter He had created into the things that pleased Him, thus giving the cosmos its particular frame. These words are combined to describe God's creative work in Genesis 2:3, "Then God blessed the seventh day and sanctified it, because in it He rested from all His work which God had created and made." These last words can be literally translated "created to make."

1. Suppose that you possessed no other revelation about God than the first two chapters of Genesis. What could you conclude about the character, interests, and capacities of the Creator?

2. No arguments are set forward to prove the existence of God in the beginning. God is simply the first subject of the first sentence. Yet we write books and convene conferences to prove the existence of God today. What do you make of this contrast between our contemporary interest in proving God's existence and the ancient text, which makes no attempt to prove His existence?

::THE IMAGE OF LIGHT

The very first words spoken by God are, "Let there be light." It is no wonder, then, that light becomes a dominant metaphor throughout the rest of Scripture for concepts like divine presence (John 1:1-9), knowledge (1 John 1:5-7), and salvation (Revelation 21:22-27). Perhaps the first words of God should form a regular prayer of yours, "O send out Your light and Your truth, let them lead me" (Psalm 43:3).

3. Jewish sages noted that each of the first three days of Creation finds its complement in the subsequent three days. Using the chart below, take note of what is created and what you discover about the creation or Creator on each day:

PREPARING THE UNIVERSE AS A HOME	FILLING THE UNIVERSE AS A HOME
Day One	Day Four
Day Two	Day Five
Day Three	Day Six

::CREATION FOCUSED ON MAN

On day four of Creation, the writer of Genesis lets us in on a great mystery. The lights of the heavens were to "be for signs and for seasons and for days and years" (1:14). We should stop to ask, "Signs for whom?" Although man had not yet been created, the heavens were being fashioned for him. God established the cosmos as a home for man, who would read the signs (and seasons, days, and years) by the revolution of the heavenly bodies.

4. In the whole array of creation, only one creature was fashioned "in the image of God." What responsibilities and capabilities did God give to Adam, traits that set him apart from the rest of the created order?

While the opening chapters of Genesis are cosmic in their scope, they are personal in their implications. How has your reading influenced your sense of self-worth before God and your perspective of belonging in His universe?

::PREJUDICE IMPERILED

If you accept the authority of the Bible, all forms of racial prejudice become untenable. All other animals in the sky, sea, and land were created "according to their kinds." There is, however, only one kind of creature called *man*. According to the Mishnah — the authoritative compilation of Jewish oral law — Adam was created alone, as the sole progenitor of the whole human race, so that no one could say to another, "My father is greater than your father" (Sanhedrin 4:5).[3] Thus, no one group of people can claim superiority over another. As the prophet Malachi put it, "Do we not all have one father? Has not one God created us?" (2:10).

5. When God created the cosmos, He didn't spin a thousand *autonomous* entities into existence; rather, He created a system of ordered *interrelationships*. What is stated or implied about each of the following interrelationships?

GOD AND THE COSMOS	HUMANITY AND THE EARTH
GOD AND HUMANITY	**MAN AND WOMAN**

6. How can you practically and purposefully improve on the relationships God designed you for: Your relationship with the earth? Your relationship with your family members or spouse? Your relationship with your Creator?

When God spoke into nothingness and said, "Let there be light," it was so. When He separated the seas from the dry land, it was good. But when He rested from all His work on the seventh day, the work was not finished. Indeed, God had finished *His* part of the work (2:2), but the ongoing work of creation had just begun.

7. How do the plants and animals carry on the work of creation?

   How do humans carry out the ongoing, creative work of God in the cosmos?

   In regard to your own God-given strengths and interests, how might you participate in the ongoing, creative work of God?

8. Genesis 2:10-14 describes a river that waters Eden, which then divides into four separate channels as it flows out of the garden. What does this detail suggest about the connection between Eden and the rest of earth?

::FOLLOW THE RIVER'S COURSE

In the book of Ezekiel, we read how the prophet had a vision of a life-giving river flowing from God's presence in the temple, bringing life to everything it touches (47:8-11, ESV). John saw the same river flowing from God's throne in heaven, bringing healing for the nations (Revelation 22:1-2). You might say that the river of life continued to flow from Eden into eternity!

9. When God searched for a helper suitable for the first man, He paraded all the other animals before Adam. Why do you think He did this?

   Describe the real and felt connection between Adam and Eve.

::ONE SMALL PROBLEM

Writing more than fifty years before the birth of Christ, Lucretius insisted that "this world has been made by nature, just as the seeds of things [i.e. atoms] have chanced spontaneously to clash, after being brought together in manifold wise without purpose, without foresight."[4] The only serious challenge to the worldview of this brilliant, ancient materialist was the mind and soul of man. About these, he conceded, "I am unable at present to set forth [their] hidden causes."[5] The only problem we run into if we attempt to dismiss or discredit the notion of the divine image in man is . . . the divine image in man.

A NEW TESTAMENT EXCURSION

Read John 1:1-14.

When the apostle John began his gospel narrative about the life and teachings of Jesus, he opted for a highly stylized prologue to take the reader back to the opening chapters of Genesis.

1. How does the word choice and imagery of this introduction remind you of the account of Creation in Genesis?

2. What role did "the Word" play in creating the cosmos? ("The Word" is specifically identified as "the only Son from the Father" in verse 14, ESV.)

3. How would you restate in your own words the ironic tension John describes between the Word's authority over the world and the world's reception of the Word?

Now read Hebrews 11:1-3.

Consider how someone would urge a persecution-weary church to hold fast to the faith they originally professed. The writer of Hebrews opted to do so by presenting example after example of men and women in the Bible who related to God on the basis of tenacious faith. Before the writer gave any example of how others have demonstrated fidelity to God, though, he began by saying, "By faith we understand that the worlds were prepared by the word of God" (11:3).

4. Why do you suppose belief in the doctrine of Creation stands at the head of this list of examples of faithful people?

5. How would you describe the relationship between believing and understanding indicated in Hebrews 11:3?

6. How might a believer's understanding of the Creator and the cosmos shape his or her response to suffering or persecution?

REFLECTIONS

Many people today are troubled by the suggestion that something was created *out of nothing*. They do not seem equally mystified by the notion that something was created *instead of* nothing.

1. Pause and ponder the following questions: Why did God make anything at all? Why did He create me? How would you answer these questions now that you have studied Genesis 1 and 2?

There are multiple stories—scientific and religious—that attempt to explain the origin of the cosmos. Choose one of these alternative explanations and consider the following questions:

2. How is it distinct from the biblical account you have studied?

3. Is it incompatible in whole or in part with the biblical version?

4. What are (or could be) the consequences of adopting a contrasting account of the origins of the world and of humanity?

::PERSONAL SIGNIFICANCE IN THE COSMIC VOID

For many people in the modern era, the vastness of the universe makes the prospect of a personal God seem unlikely. "Now that we know how insignificant our planet is," the argument goes, "how could we possibly suppose there is a God watching over us who is interested in a personal relationship with individuals?"

It might be helpful to point a person who holds such a view to Ptolemy's *Almagest*—an astronomical treatise composed more than a hundred years after Christ's ascension. In three short proofs, the author concludes that "the Earth has the Ratio of a Point to the Heavens" (Almagest 1, 6).[6] King David had made the same observation in a more personal way centuries before Ptolemy by asking, "When I consider Your heavens . . . what is man?" (Psalm 8:3-4). The thinkers in antiquity were well aware of the vast emptiness of the heavens and the virtual insignificance of humanity relative to it. Yet somehow they found it possible to believe they were more than atomic accidents floating atop an unremarkable rock around an insignificant star.

INTERSECTIONS

The story of Job is one of the most poignant and probing dramas in the Bible. In it we learn that one man can be the focal point of a cosmic conflict between God and Satan—and that somehow the archenemy of God loses if one man will hold fast to his faith in the face of severe affliction.[7] At the end of thirty-seven chapters, Job has lost everything—his property, family, and dignity—and it appears that he might indeed lose his faith as he grows increasingly defiant of God. But then God shows up to answer Job. Read Job 38:1–42:6 and consider:

1. In a few sentences, how would you summarize God's reply to Job?

2. List the kinds of things over which God exerts creative or sustaining force in the cosmos.

3. What words would you use to describe Job's response to God?

G. K. Chesterton commented that "the more we really look at man as an animal, the less he will look like one."[8] Apparently, the directors of the London Zoo failed to consider this point when they sponsored a special event designed to "teach members of the public that the human is just another primate." In the summer of 2005, the zoo opened an exhibit featuring *Homo sapiens* in fig leaves, sitting in a cage, picking at one another's hair. There was one problem with this publicity event: the *Homo sapiens* in the cage were not acting like *Homo sapiens* at all.

4. Using all your powers of imagination and irony, mentally redesign this exhibit in your mind with *Homo sapiens* truly acting like humans. What would they be wearing, discussing, and doing?

LAY IT TO YOUR HEART

Meditate on these passages and commit them to memory:

- By the word of the LORD the heavens were made, and by the breath of His mouth all their host. (Psalm 33:6)
- Do we not all have one father? Has not one God created us? (Malachi 2:10)
- By faith we understand that the worlds were prepared by the word of God, so that what is seen was not made out of things which are visible. (Hebrews 11:3)

:: 2

THE GRAVITY OF OUR FALL

HUMANITY'S PLUMMET FROM PERFECTION TO IMPERFECTION ::

When God generated the universe, He set it up to operate according to natural laws. The velocity of light (*c* in scientific notation, as in $E=mc^2$) is a universal constant. It would not do to call it a constant if the velocity of light could be 299,792 kilometers per second today and 299,782 kilometers per second tomorrow. The universe operates by law, not chance. The divine will to bring cosmos out of chaos makes all scientific endeavor meaningful.

But what scientist or theologian could have ever predicted that the second law of thermodynamics in the world of nature would have had a spiritual counterpart in the heart of humans. Entropy is increasing in the universe!

At this point, you may be regretting that you paid so little attention in physics class. "What in the world is *entropy*?" you may be asking.

Entropy is the measure of disorder in a closed natural system. The second law of thermodynamics assures us that things will always proceed from a state of *more* to *less* order in a closed system unless acted on by some outside force. Order will naturally move toward disorder.

Should you question the validity of this law, simply remove all adult supervision from the toddler nursery at your church next Sunday morning. Or watch what happens to the typical house if the owner doesn't repair the roof, apply fresh paint when needed, and fix plumbing leaks.

What we discover in Genesis 3 and beyond is that entropy's effects in the natural world are mirrored in the spiritual world also. But where did it all begin? There is no suggestion of spiritual disorder in Eden, no reason to suppose that the human soul or human society *had* to fall into spiritual disarray.

So what went wrong? How did the cosmic harmony of the first two chapters of Genesis devolve into turmoil? Things were going so well. . . . What happened?

These answers can be found in Genesis 3 to 7. And though somewhat mysterious and unflattering to the children of Adam, they are the only means we have of making any sense of the human condition—the good, the bad, and the ugly. We see that sin entered the world, and when it did, the results were devastating.

Blaise Pascal said, "Certainly, nothing offends us more rudely than this doctrine [of original sin]; and yet, without this mystery, the most incomprehensible of all, we are incomprehensible to ourselves. The knowledge of our condition takes its twists and turns in this abyss, so that man is more inconceivable without this mystery than this mystery is inconceivable to man."[1]

To understand the biblical portrait of the Fall is to understand ourselves, our world, our adversary, and our only hope for salvation. To ignore it is to plunge headlong into the self-centered desolation of spiritual entropy that Adam and Eve found themselves in before God set them aright by His revelation.

THE OPEN ROAD

Read Genesis 3–4; 6–7.

:: "SERPENT" = "SATAN"

Why do we identify the serpent in the garden with Satan? Because Paul and John do in their writings (see Romans 16:20 and Revelation 12:9). Accordingly, we may say that Genesis 3:15 preaches the gospel in advance . . . if only in outline.

1. Consider the "anatomy of temptation" as described in Genesis 3:1-6. What does the serpent insinuate about the character of God?

   How does he misrepresent God's words?

2. We often fall prey to the same temptations of Satan time and again. (He seems to know our weak spots.) What aspect of God's character does Satan most often seek to mislead you about?

3. How would you describe the nature of Adam and Eve's sin? *What* did they do wrong?

How do you account for the choice they made? *Why* did they do wrong?

::HALF-TRUTH = TOTAL DESTRUCTION

Satan damned humanity with a half-truth. He promised that Adam and Eve would become like God when they ate from the Tree of the Knowledge of Good and Evil, and that's what happened (Genesis 3:22). Like God, man now knows good and evil. But unlike God, man does not possess the wisdom or strength to master his evil inclinations (4:7).

4. Observe the immediate aftereffects of Adam and Eve's sin in Genesis 3:8-21. What do you notice about the following?:

THEIR SENSE OF SELF-AWARENESS	THEIR CONVERSATION WITH GOD	GOD'S RESPONSE TO ADAM AND EVE

5. Describe a time when you sensed God confronting you about a sin. Did you feel exposed? Did you try to hide from Him? How did you hear God walking toward you and calling your name? Did you respond to Him immediately . . . or eventually?

::DOUBLE JEOPARDY

When Adam and Eve sinned, their eyes were opened to their nakedness; they felt ashamed of themselves and scared of God. The Fall wrecked them internally. When God cursed man in Genesis 3:14-19, he added external hardships in the world, such as pain in childbirth and thorny soil. Thus, in one act, man forfeited harmony with God and inherited hardship on the earth.

6. Why did God evict Adam and Eve from the garden?

   How might human history have been different if God had not set a limit to sinful man's lifespan?

7. Have you seen a person respond to the voice of the Lord when faced with the reality of death? How might a person's relationship to sin change if he or she remained consistently aware of life's brevity?

::THE CHERUBIM

In biblical cosmology, the *cherubim* (Hebrew plural for "cherub") are angelic warriors, not pudgy child-angels with golden bells. God placed cherubim and a flaming sword at the east of Eden to guard the way to the Tree of Life, so that fallen man would not live forever and make all creation a living hell. We hear nothing of the angelic warriors again until Exodus 25, when God instructs Moses that two golden cherubim should be fashioned atop the ark of the covenant. At the ark, under the outspread wings of the cherubim, people could find atonement for their sins and direction from the Law. Thus, the cherubim at the gate of Eden cut sinful people off from the source of eternal life, until the time when another pair of cherubim atop the ark gazed down at where it might be found.

8. When God banished Adam and Eve from the garden, He did not withdraw His presence from them altogether. Far from it. What does Scripture tell us about the relationship God maintained with the first family after the Fall?

   How does Eve speak about God upon the birth of her children in the first verses of Genesis 4?

9. Genesis 4:3 indicates that "in the course of time," Cain and Abel brought offerings to the Lord. What does this detail suggest about the relationship the Lord maintained with Cain and Abel?

10. Describe Cain's reaction to God when his offering is rejected.

What warning does God give Cain?

Characterize Cain's attitude toward God when he is called to account for Abel's murder (Genesis 4:5-10).

11. Genesis 6 picks up the story about 1,600 years after Adam and Eve left the Garden of Eden. (Engage your powers of historical imagination to consider how much human history transpires in that amount of time.) Consider and answer the following questions:

HOW IS HUMANITY CHARACTERIZED?	HOW IS NOAH CHARACTERIZED?
WHAT IS GOD'S RESPONSE TO HUMANITY?	**WHAT IS GOD'S RESPONSE TO NOAH?**

::AFTER THE FLOOD, A COVENANT

Before reading further, see if you can identify the seven laws implied in God's covenant with Noah after he left the ark (see Genesis 8:20–9:17). Jewish sages believe that God will hold the whole Gentile world accountable to these laws, which were given to restrain people from the madness and violence that had swept over the earth prior to the flood. The laws relate to (1) idolatry, (2) cursing the Lord, (3) murder, (4) sexual transgression, (5) theft, (6) establishing a court system, and (7) eating meat with blood in it.

12. Revisit your notes above (and in the previous chapter) and consider the following: If you had only the accounts of Adam and Eve, Cain, and Noah to go on, what knowledge would you have about . . .

THE EFFECTS OF SIN IN THE LIFE OF HUMANS?	GOD'S RESPONSE TO SIN?	THE CHARACTER AND CAPABILITIES OF GOD?

13. What have you learned about the nature of sin in your own life as you have reflected on Genesis 3–7? How does your understanding of your sin affect your sense of standing before God?

:: EVIL WITHIN

The famous Russian writer Aleksandr Solzhenitsyn once said, "If only there were evil people somewhere insidiously committing evil deeds, and it were necessary only to separate them from the rest of us and destroy them. But the line dividing good and evil cuts through the heart of every human being. And who is willing to destroy a piece of his own heart?"[2]

A NEW TESTAMENT EXCURSION

Read Romans 5:12-19.

Knowing what we know about Adam, very few of us would have voted for him to serve as our first representative before God. However, we didn't get to vote. God made that call for us providentially. What is more, He also graciously decreed that Jesus would stand as our representative for redemption. In Romans 5:12-19, Paul compares the representational influence that both Adam and Jesus exert over all humans.

1. How does Paul describe the influence of Adam's life on all of us?

2. Compare the influence of Jesus' life to that of Adam's?

3. In what ways does the "free gift" of Jesus differ from the "transgression" of Adam?

Now take a look at 2 Peter 2:1-9.

What could be worse than a lie? How about a lie that leads Christians into sensuality, arrogance, ignorance, and apostasy? That was the peril facing the church in Peter's day, and so the apostle wrote to steer the church clear of destructive heresies.

4. What three examples from the Old Testament did Peter use to warn the church about God's judgment against sin?

5. What do all three of the examples have in common?

6. Describe in your own words the pattern of judgment and salvation outlined in this passage.

REFLECTIONS

Nothing inherent in the fruit of the Tree of the Knowledge of Good and Evil rendered it wrong for Adam and Eve to eat. Only by virtue of His command did God make an indifferent matter a moral one. In other words, there was nothing bad about the *fruit*—but there was something bad about the *choice* to eat the fruit when God had prohibited doing so.

God may do something similar in His relationship with you. He may direct you to give up a habit or make a particular choice that may not be an issue of right and wrong for the rest of the world but only for you.

1. Have you ever sensed God convicting you in this way in the past? What about the present?

2. In what ways might God be leading you to lay down a sinful habit or take up a constructive one?

3. The apostle James wrote, "Therefore, to one who knows the right thing to do and does not do it, to him it is sin" (4:17). Restate and personalize this principle in your own words.

In the song "Imagine," John Lennon asked us to conceive of a human society relieved of any sense of accountability to heaven. Without a need for religion or a belief in the afterlife, Lennon envisioned a borderless brotherhood of man where tranquility and equality reign.

4. How does the picture of a godless society in Genesis 6 contrast with Lennon's vision?

5. How might our modern emphasis on the promise of technology, education, or political reform *without* reference to God work to the detriment of a society?

INTERSECTIONS

How does it feel to be forgiven? What does it mean to have your transgressions covered? David, the great poet-king of Israel, knew the answers to these questions from personal experience and theological reflection. He wrote Psalm 32 with these questions in mind.

1. According to this psalm, what are the effects of harboring unconfessed sin?

2. Describe the life-change that occurred when the psalmist acknowledged his sin to the Lord.

Ray Comfort, a prominent contemporary evangelist, says Christians should never present the gospel without making it clear that everyone stands under the judgment of God against sin. (Visit www.livingwaters.com/listenwatch.shtml to access Comfort's lecture entitled "Hell's Best Kept Secret," which was available at the time of this writing.)

3. Why might believers avoid or soft-sell the issue of sin when sharing the gospel?

4. Do you agree with Comfort that nonbelievers should be told up front about God's judgment against sinful behavior?

LAY IT TO YOUR HEART

Meditate on these passages and commit them to memory:

- There is no one who does not sin. (1 Kings 8:46, ESV)
- All these evil things proceed from within and defile the man. (Mark 7:23)
- To one who knows the right thing to do and does not do it, to him it is sin. (James 4:17)

::3

ONE FAMILY FOR ALL NATIONS

GOD'S CHOSEN PEOPLE OPEN A NEW CHAPTER IN HISTORY ::

In the early chapters of the Bible, two thousand years of human history are summed up by reporting primarily on the lives of two men—Adam and Noah—and their families. That same pattern carries on as the focus of attention shifts to another man, Abraham, and his descendants.[1] In fact, it is fair to say that the rest of the Bible—indeed, the rest of human history—is concerned primarily with this one man and his offspring.

Who must this man of divine significance be? What international stature or personal distinction could he claim?

We pick up his story in Genesis when he is an older, upper-middle-class migrant, who wandered from Persia to Palestine to Egypt and back to Palestine again in his lifetime. The only plot of land he ever owns is a cave in which to bury his wife, who doesn't come off in the text as a model of virtue or discretion.

In short, Abraham hardly cuts the figure of a hero. And yet, he is counted as the father of the Jewish nation, the direct ancestor of the

Messiah, and the forebear of all who have believed in Jesus. What is more, God Himself calls this man "My friend" (Isaiah 41:8). Why? What is it about Abraham that he should be the father of God's chosen people?

There seems to be only one meaningful answer: He trusted tenaciously in God.

Abraham had extraordinary faith in the promises God made to him. The man simply would not doubt, or be deterred in any way, when the Lord told him He'd do something.

Now, it is quite evident that Abraham made a few mistakes along the way, mistakes that generally found him trying to "assist" God in bringing His promises to pass. Invariably, though, Abraham learned through hardship that God does not need our assistance, instead He requires total obedience flowing from a heart of faith.

As you open up the Scriptures, consider how miraculous a move it was for God to magnify His expansive love to all the nations through the offspring of this one, otherwise nondescript, migrant from Babylon.

THE OPEN ROAD

Read Genesis 12–17.

1. Sages have called the era of human history from Genesis 3–11 "the Age of Desolation" (consider 6:5-7 and 11:8-9). Why do you think this two-thousand-year period earned such a bleak designation?

2. What did God do to dispel the desolation and inaugurate a new era in Genesis 12:1-9?

3. How were Abraham and his descendants to fare because of God's covenant? What about the families of the nations?

:: WHAT WOULD ABRAHAM DO?

According to the Jewish commentator Nachmanides (c. 1194–1270), "Whatever happened to the Patriarchs is a portent [a sign] for the children."[2] Abraham's life was not merely a history but a foreshadowing of the faith-filled response God desires to see in each of us. Thus, Jesus challenged His hard-hearted detractors with these words: "If you are Abraham's children, do the deeds of Abraham. But as it is, you are seeking to kill Me, a man who has told you the truth, which I heard from God; this Abraham did not do" (John 8:39-40).

4. How would you describe Abraham's devotion to God when he was called away from Haran and traveled about in Canaan (Genesis 12:4-9)?

5. What contrasts do you observe in his behavior in Egypt (12:10-20)?

How do you account for this contrast?

6. What circumstances in your life compel you to respond in fear and self-protection rather than faith?

When Abraham returned to Canaan from Egypt, he and Lot were simply unable to reside in close proximity to one another any longer. Their herds were too numerous and their herdsmen too contentious to graze the same pastures. Abraham could have taken the pick of the land by virtue of his age and position, but he deferred to Lot, who chose to move eastward into the fertile Jordan River valley.

7. How did Lot's fortunes shift as he moved away from Canaan, the Promised Land?

What lessons or warnings are suggested by Lot's fate?

:: CENSURING THE CENSUS

Because of God's promise to Abraham in Genesis 13:16, 15:5, and 22:17 that his descendants would be innumerable, it was considered a presumptuous sin to take a direct headcount of all Israel. An indirect method of census-taking is described in Exodus 30:11-16. A *partial* headcount census is described in Numbers 1. And the disastrous effects of a full headcount census under King David are described in 2 Samuel 24.

8. Genesis 14 paints a picture of Abraham's involvement in a regional war in Canaan. How would you characterize Abraham's influence among the leaders of these tribes?

   What was the nature of the vow that Abraham had made to the Lord, a vow that led him to decline accepting any of the spoils of war?

   What does Abraham's vow suggest about his relationship to the Lord?

9. In Genesis 15, we find God clearly affirming His covenant with Abraham yet again. Survey the several instances where God states His covenant with Abraham and complete the chart that follows:

PASSAGE	WHAT DOES GOD PROMISE?	WHO ARE THE BENEFICIARIES?
Genesis 12:2-3,7		
Genesis 13:14-17		
Genesis 15:1-6,13-18		
Genesis 17:1-8		

10. The Scriptures teach that those who share in the faith of Abraham are heirs *according to* these promises and heirs *of* these promises (see, for example, Romans 4). What portion of the promises above do you long to see fulfilled in your own life?

:: SEALING A COVENANT

In Old Testament times, a promise was considered binding when two parties passed between the halves of an animal sacrifice. (See, for example, Jeremiah 34:17-20.)

11. Throughout Genesis 12–17, Abraham faces many circumstances that make it seem unlikely God's promises will ever be fulfilled. List three such obstacles and note how Abraham responds to them:

    a.

    b.

    c.

12. Describe the problems that arise in Genesis 16 when Abraham and Sarah act to "assist" God in bringing His promise to fulfillment. What are the immediate and long-term consequences?

13. Have you encountered any circumstances when God was not working out His will on your timetable or in your way? Have practical circumstances ever seemed irreconcilable with divine promises? How did (or might) you counter the temptation to "help" God along by taking matters into your own hands when such circumstances arise?

::RIGHTEOUSNESS, REALITY, AND THE RESURRECTION

Though the Old Testament does not have a strong emphasis on life-after-death teaching, it does offer a clear promise from God that the righteous will be blessed and the wicked punished. It doesn't take special intellect to observe, however, that the wicked often prosper throughout life and the righteous suffer harm and privation (see Jeremiah 12:1-2, for instance). How is one to reconcile God's clear promise with the equally clear refutation of real-life experience? Simple: This is not the only "real life" we will experience. Another life beyond this one exists where the promised blessings for righteousness and curses for wickedness will be fulfilled. Real existence cannot terminate at the grave for, as Jesus says, "The Scripture cannot be broken" (John 10:35).

A NEW TESTAMENT EXCURSION

Read Romans 4.

Because of Christianity's close link with Judaism, many first-century Jewish Christians believed that Gentiles who decided to follow Jesus needed to adhere to the Law of Moses to be counted as God's chosen people. Paul looks back to Abraham's life to argue his case against this doctrine (see also Galatians 3:1-14).

1. On what basis was Abraham considered righteous by God?

2. On what basis did God make promises to bless Abraham (and all nations)?

3. Was the Mosaic Law known during Abraham's lifetime?

4. In what way do these lessons from Abraham's account influence how you think about attaining a righteous standing before God? How do the lessons influence your thinking about your relation to the Mosaic Law?

::THE GOSPEL ACCORDING TO ABRAHAM

In Galatians 3:7-9, Paul referred to God's promise to Abraham in Genesis 12:2-3, saying Scripture "preached the gospel beforehand." From the beginning, God chose Abraham — the man of faith — in order to bless the people of all nations who would share in that same faith.

Now take a look at Ephesians 2:11-22.

In this passage, Paul establishes a Christian framework for answering this question: Who can be called God's chosen people now that Gentiles have come to believe in the Messiah? Consider how Paul describes the condition of Gentiles apart from Christ (or prior to the time of the Messiah) and their condition in Christ.

GENTILES APART FROM CHRIST	GENTILES IN CHRIST

REFLECTIONS

Among other things, Abraham's story teaches us that it is not *our commitments to God* but *His commitments to us* that make the greatest difference in life. The spiritual significance of our life does not originate in our faithfulness to God but in His faithfulness to His promises and His unrelenting love for us.

1. How might our perspective on God and our experience of daily life be altered if we held this distinction in mind?

2. How can you more decisively and consciously live according to the commitments God has made to you?

If you approached the average person on the street with the claim that Christians (or Jews) are God's chosen people, chances are you would not find a favorable hearing. Notions like this offend our culture's strong push to be inclusive, egalitarian, and tolerant.

3. How might you converse with a nonreligious friend about this idea without sounding like you're slamming the door of salvation on the rest of humanity?

4. How does Genesis 12–17 attest to the breadth of God's concern for all people?

5. How might Jesus' answer to a similar question (see Luke 13:22-30) inform your approach?

INTERSECTIONS

In Malachi 3:6, the Lord proclaimed, "I, the Lord, do not change; therefore you, O sons of Jacob, are not consumed." When God chose Abraham and his descendants to inherit Canaan and bless the nations, He made an eternal commitment that profoundly influenced all His subsequent dealings with Israel. Because the Lord would not retract His covenant with Abraham, Israel knew that God would never utterly forsake them.

Examine the following passages and make a note of the circumstances in which Israel found favor and deliverance because of God's covenant with Abraham:

- Exodus 6:2-9

- 2 Kings 13:22-23

- Luke 1:67-75

At the account of Ishmael, Abraham's son through Hagar, Muslims part company with Jews and Christians in their view of salvation history. While Ishmael is a minor character in the Bible, he is revered as a prophet in Islam and a forebear of Muhammad. In an effort to better understand his place in Islamic belief, search an encyclopedia (such as www.wikipedia.com) for an entry on Ishmael. It is interesting to observe the areas where Muslim traditions and the biblical narrative diverge. The story of Hagar and Ishmael is memorialized during the Hajj, the religious pilgrimage to Mecca.

1. What value do you see in understanding the similarities and differences among the Islamic, Jewish, and Christian faiths?

2. Do you have a Muslim friend who could tell you more about which persons from the Bible are recognized as prophets in Islam?

LAY IT TO YOUR HEART

Meditate on these passages and commit them to memory:

- [Abraham] believed in the LORD; and He reckoned it to him as righteousness. (Genesis 15:6)
- Be sure that it is those who are of faith who are sons of Abraham. (Galatians 3:7)
- So then you are no longer strangers and aliens, but you are fellow citizens with the saints, and are of God's household. (Ephesians 2:19)

:: 4

SHATTERING THE YOKE OF SLAVERY

DIVINE DELIVERANCE FROM THE SEVEREST TRIALS ::

The book of *beginnings*, Genesis, ends with the descendants of Abraham settling down in Egypt, having fled the Promised Land because of a severe drought. The book of *deliverance*, Exodus, opens up with an overview of Israel's fall from fortune into bitter slavery in Egypt, a period covering just over two hundred years.

The chosen people had grown from a modest extended family of seventy to a nation too many and too mighty for Egypt's comfort (see Exodus 1:9). Thus, the rulers of Egypt did what they could to contain and eventually reduce the population of Israel, finally resorting to infanticide when their program of forced labor was failing.

Yet even in this dark hour, God turned an evil design into a hallmark of His redemptive power. One Hebrew baby was spared the sentence of death-by-drowning in the Nile to be brought up in the palace of the Pharaoh. Later in life, that same individual—Moses—would come back to overturn the empire and deliver the people of Israel from bondage.

Every culture maintains a repository of tales about how the nation was founded or preserved against extraordinary odds. But there is nothing in the annals of human history like the Exodus of Israel from Egypt. An entire nation of battered slaves—"six hundred thousand men on foot, aside from children" (Exodus 12:37)—simply walked across the threshold of the mightiest empire in the world on their way home. They carried with them the treasures of their oppressors, the memory of cruel servitude, and the hope of a better tomorrow in Canaan, the Promised Land.

No wonder this act of salvation—so comprehensive and so incomprehensible—sets the benchmark for all future acts of divine deliverance.

As you read through the Bible, you begin to discover that every act of deliverance is referenced back to the Exodus. Even Jesus, the Messiah, finds harbor in Egypt and is called out again, escaping a program of infanticide so that His story might echo the divine pattern God inaugurated in the text you are about to study (see Matthew 2:13-20). And should the pattern surrounding the Messiah's birth be missed, the explicit language about His death cannot be: "For Christ our Passover also has been sacrificed" (1 Corinthians 5:7). The doctrine of deliverance taught in fullness in the New Testament finds its origins in the Exodus.

THE OPEN ROAD

Read Exodus 2:23–6:12; 11–14.

1. How does God respond to Israel's plight, according to Exodus 2:24-25?

   God *heard* . . .

God *remembered* . . .

God *saw* . . .

God *took notice* . . .

2. What does this passage suggest to you about God's providence and character?

3. Has there been a time in your life when you wondered if God knew or cared what you were going through? How does this passage influence your perspective on that time?

::DELIVERANCE ON ITS WAY

Sages say that the bitterest period of bondage for Israel occurred during the eighty-six years before Moses returned to Egypt. No doubt this era of ruthless slavery would have been the time Israel cried out to God most fervently for deliverance. God responded immediately to these cries, sparing Moses from execution eighty years before he arrived back at the palace to secure the freedom of his people (see Exodus 7:7).

When Moses was perhaps forty years old, he had attempted to step up and deliver Israel—or at least one Israelite—from Egyptian injustice. The move almost cost him his life, and Moses was forced to flee to Midian, beyond the reach of Pharaoh's empire. God met Moses again at the beginning of Exodus 3 with a shocking and not-altogether welcome invitation.

4. In what way did God reveal Himself to Moses in Exodus 3:1-9?

   How did God identify Himself?

   Why do you think God appeared to Moses when He did?

5. Reflect on the five objections Moses raised to God's summons in Exodus 3:10–4:17.

MOSES' OBJECTION	WHAT ISSUES OR INSECURITIES WERE CONFOUNDING MOSES?	HOW DOES GOD RESPOND TO MOSES?
"Who am I, that I should go to Pharaoh, and that I should bring the sons of Israel out of Egypt?" (3:11)		

MOSES' OBJECTION	WHAT ISSUES OR INSECURITIES WERE CONFOUNDING MOSES?	HOW DOES GOD RESPOND TO MOSES?
"Behold, I am going to the sons of Israel, and I will say to them, 'The God of your fathers has sent me to you.' Now they may say to me, 'What is His name?' What shall I say to them?" (3:13)		
"What if they will not believe me or listen to what I say? For they may say, 'The Lord has not appeared to you.'" (4:1)		
"Please, Lord, I have never been eloquent, neither recently nor in time past, nor since You have spoken to Your servant; for I am slow of speech and slow of tongue." (4:10)		

MOSES' OBJECTION	WHAT ISSUES OR INSECURITIES WERE CONFOUNDING MOSES?	HOW DOES GOD RESPOND TO MOSES?
"Please, Lord, now send the message by whomever You will [i.e., please send someone else]." (4:13)		

6. Has God ever led you into a situation you felt inadequate to handle? Can you relate to the objections Moses brought before God? How do God's responses to Moses apply to circumstances you've faced?

After Moses failed to convince the Almighty that He made a big mistake, the reluctant messenger teamed up with his brother, Aaron, and proceeded to Egypt to proclaim God's message to Pharaoh.

7. Consider the outcome of Moses' first interview with Pharaoh (Exodus 5:1–6:12). How does Pharaoh react?

What are the immediate repercussions for the Israelite people?

How do the Israelites respond to Moses?

8. Draw out five lessons on leadership from Moses' life before God delivered the Israelites out of Egypt:

   a.

   b.

   c.

   d.

   e.

9. In Exodus 11–12, God tells Moses—and Moses tells Pharaoh—that a final, deadly plague will strike Egypt. (God had offered nine portentous signs already, but Pharaoh had been unwilling to release his slaves.) What would be the tenth and final plague?

According to 12:29-33, what effect did the tenth plague have on Pharaoh's resolve?

::MEASURE FOR MEASURE

Scriptures teach that God multiplies back to the unrepentant what they have dealt out in unrighteousness (for example, see Psalm 9:15-16, Jeremiah 14:15, Joel 3:5-8, and Obadiah 1:15). Pharaoh had attempted to reduce the number of Israelites by murdering their firstborn sons. God responded to this evil act by sending the death angel to slay all the firstborn males in Pharaoh's kingdom. In the words of a later prophet, Pharaoh sowed the wind and harvested the whirlwind (see Hosea 8:7).

Before God sent the death angel throughout Egypt to execute His final judgment, He told Israel how to avert the judgment. In addition, He also provided direction as to how future generations were to memorialize this astounding act of deliverance.

10. How were the Israelites to observe the *first* Passover (Exodus 12:3-13,21-28)?

Why did they do so?

How was the Passover to be celebrated *in the future* (12:14-20,43-49; 13:3-10)? Why?

By what process were the Israelites to consecrate their firstborn males (13:1-2,11-16)?

Why were they to do this?

11. In the Passover celebration God's people perpetually reflect on their salvation. In what ways do you (or could you) regularly reflect on your own deliverance "from the domain of darkness" and your transfer "to the kingdom of His beloved Son" (Colossians 1:13)?

::THE FIRST AND FOREMOST COMMANDMENT

Sandwiched between the threat of the tenth plague and the instructions for surviving it, Exodus 12:2 is easy to . . . *pass over.* To do so, however, would be to miss the *first* commandment given to the nation of Israel and the *foremost* ordinance regulating their religious life. God called the chosen people of Israel to establish their monthly calendars around the appearance of the new moon. The word *chodesh* in this verse can be interpreted "month" or "renewal" (that is, renewal of the moon). All of Israel's religious holidays were to be determined by the lunar calendar. Thus, God oriented their annual festivals around the time of His miraculous redemption from Egypt.

12. What observations do you make about the following means God used to lead the Israelites out of Egypt?

    Taking the long route to avoid immediate war with the Philistines (13:17-18).

    Directing their way with a pillar of cloud by day and fire by night (13:21-22; 14:19-20).

    Turning them back to square off against Pharaoh's army (14:1-4).

    Parting the Red Sea as a path for Israel and a grave for Pharaoh's army (14:15-31).

13. What principles from these verses inspire or encourage you to trust the Lord's leading, even if His path is hard to understand?

::HUMILIATION IN HISTORY?

Skeptical modern scholars doubt that two to three million Jews departed *en masse* from Egypt. They ask, "How could such an extraordinary event fail to be recorded in the annals of Egyptian history?" Perhaps the rulers of Egypt chose not to memorialize a monumental national embarrassment. It is one thing to carve scenes of a defeat in battle on your pyramid walls; it's another thing to record the calamitous loss of millions of destitute slaves whose God somehow managed to plunder your country and wash away your king's cavalry.

A NEW TESTAMENT EXCURSION

Read Acts 7.

Asked to explain his allegiance to Jesus, Stephen delivered this stunning speech before the Jewish high court, the Sanhedrin, which had condemned Jesus to death only weeks before. Stephen defended himself by reminding the Sanhedrin of the ways God had delivered Israel from Egypt.

1. From Acts 7, list five references to events you have studied in Genesis or Exodus:

    a.

b.

c.

d.

e.

2. Let us assume that Stephen was not trying to filibuster the Sanhedrin and delay his sentence by rehearsing so much Old Testament history. What was the point to his soliloquy, and what was the pattern he identified from Old Testament Scriptures?

Now take a look at Mark 14:12-26.

3. Think about our discussion regarding the Passover. Describe what the twelve disciples were likely doing as they prepared the Passover for Jesus and themselves.

4. What connections do you see between the symbolism of the Passover and the significance of Jesus' imminent death?

REFLECTIONS

When our computers break, we call a specialist in technical support. When our bones break, we rush to an emergency room. But when our hearts break or our lives fall apart, where do we turn for help? Often, it is not to the first expert we *should* look to—God.

1. Recall a time when you turned to someone or something other than God to find deliverance from some distress. What were the short-term and long-term consequences?

2. How might you take the lessons you have learned and the Scriptures you have studied to encourage yourself or a believing friend to turn to God during tough times?

Our world is reeling with injustice, poverty, and persecution today. Yet, billions of people are responding to these pressing needs by saying, as Moses did, "Oh, my Lord, please send someone else" (Exodus 4:13, ESV).

3. Consider how you could turn the truths from your study of Exodus into regular prayers for justice in a specific area of social concern and into active engagement in a struggle for justice. (Bear in mind that the motif of divine deliverance in Exodus has fueled some of the most radical social justice movements in contemporary history.)

   What first steps could you take? Perhaps a day of service with a local mercy ministry is in order, or a letter to a congressman expressing your concern for social action.

INTERSECTIONS

The Exodus from Egypt influenced the religious ceremonies and sacred writings of the Jews for hundreds of years. Then, in 722 and 586 BC, history repeated itself. The Jewish people found themselves ousted from the Promised Land, living as an oppressed minority in Assyria and Babylon, the dominant world powers of the time. Prophets and poets all noted the similarity this latter calamity bore to Israel's former captivity and deliverance from Egypt.

1. How does the original experience of captivity and deliverance from Egypt inform the following prayers and prophecies about Israel's "second" captivity?
   - Psalm 80
   - Jeremiah 16:9-15
   - Daniel 9

LAY IT TO YOUR HEART

Meditate on these passages and commit them to memory:

- And what one nation in the earth is like Your people Israel, whom God went to redeem for Himself as a people . . . ? (1 Chronicles 17:21)
- He brought me forth also into a broad place; He rescued me, because He delighted in me. (Psalm 18:19)
- He has delivered us from the domain of darkness and transferred us to the kingdom of his beloved Son, in whom we have redemption, the forgiveness of sins. (Colossians 1:13-14, ESV)

::5

RIGHTEOUSNESS MADE PLAIN

THE LAW ENLIGHTENS OUR PATH TOWARD LIBERTY ::

The Ten Commandments and the Bill of Rights are a lot alike. Everyone knows they're an important collections of laws. Many people can offer a rough approximation of what one or both of them say. But perhaps none of us has read the original documents more than once . . . if at all.

While this study doesn't offer much help with the Bill of Rights, it does take you right to the source of the Ten Commandments. The book of Deuteronomy records the final words of Moses as he recounts Israel's history and offers a summation of the Law God had given them on Mount Sinai.

For the people of Israel, this recap of the Law served as a point-blank reminder that, although the physical boundaries of the nation were about to change, the moral, civil, and religious boundaries had been set forty years earlier on Sinai. God had delivered Israel up from Egypt, and He was not about to deliver them over to godlessness in Canaan. The Law was to be a personal guide and a civil authority in their new land.

But why should Moses offer a restatement of the Law at all? Had he not already written four books of history and law for Israel as a reminder of God's instructions and interventions?

To begin with, it is helpful to consider that Deuteronomy is not *merely* a restatement of the Law. A close comparison of Deuteronomy to the other books of Moses reveals not only a shift in theological emphasis but also several new laws. Apparently, God intended for His people to understand the whole Law through the whole body of writings called the Torah (or Pentateuch), which is comprised of the first five books of our Old Testament.

What is more, Moses was highlighting a vital message for Israel by recounting the Law on the eastern side of the Jordan River: The revealed Law was sufficient to satisfy their spiritual hunger. Prior to entering Canaan, Israel had been guided by the fiery physical presence of God. They had been fed with food that miraculously materialized every morning like dew. The wilderness had been no Disneyland, but they had been living in a kind of magic kingdom . . . and they were about to go home.

In Canaan, the fiery presence of God would settle behind the veil of the tabernacle, and the people would farm the rich soil of Canaan for food. With their appetites whetted by miracles, what would satisfy their spiritual hunger to know and see God? Moses' answer: The Law.[1]

For a child of God today, this answer still anchors our faith. We do not rely on the magic of divine manifestations and miracles. It is enough that God "has spoken to us in His Son, whom He appointed heir of all things, through whom also He made the world" (Hebrews 1:2).

How did God speak in the past? What did He say? You'll discover the answer to these questions as you open the pages of Deuteronomy, the capstone of the Torah.

::SPELLING IT OUT

Author Philip Yancey says, "The Canaanites sacrificed children to appease their unpredictable gods. But the God of the Hebrews proved willing to sign a contract detailing exactly what he expected from his people and what he promised in return. . . . [As] Deuteronomy shows most clearly, these laws simply set the boundaries of a vastly unequal relationship: between an awesome, holy God and an ordinary people prone to failure and rebellion."[2]

THE OPEN ROAD

Read Deuteronomy 4–5; 12; 15; 17.

:: ROUND TWO

The name "Deuteronomy" comes down to us from the Greek, meaning "The Second Law" (a repetition of the Law). Jewish sages called this book the "Mishneh Torah," meaning "The Explanation of the Law." In the first four books of the Torah, God speaks directly to Moses. In Deuteronomy, the fifth and final book of the Torah, Moses reviews for Israel the instruction God had given him.

1. Moses begins his review of the Law in Deuteronomy 4 by looking back on three distinct events in Israel's recent past. What lessons from each does Moses want the people to remember and take to heart?

REMEMBER THESE EVENTS . . .	TAKE THESE LESSONS TO HEART . . .
The idolatrous affair at Baal-peor (see 4:3-4).	
The day Israel stood before the Lord to receive the Law at Horeb (see 4:10-19).	
The miraculous deliverance from Egypt (see 4:32-40).	

::IN-YOUR-FACE REMINDER

Before Moses reviewed the Law for Israel, he began with a stern warning not to turn away from the Lord. From where they were standing (Deuteronomy 3:29), the people could see Baal-peor, where the Moabites had enticed them to worship a false god and where God had broken out against them with a plague that killed 24,000 people (see Numbers 25:1-9).

2. Perhaps you have had your own "Baal-peor" experience in life, a time when you rejected God's authority and pursued your own interests. Reflect on one such time, and write down the lessons you have taken to heart from your experience.

3. Not only does Moses look to the past, asking Israel to learn from its history, but he also looks to the future, admonishing the people to remain faithful to God. According to Deuteronomy 4:25-31, what sin does Moses envision the people committing? Why do they commit it?

How will God respond to their sin?

How will God respond when they repent?

4. It is no sign of pessimism to have a plan in place for returning to God should you find yourself estranged from Him because of sin. From this passage, what practical steps could you take to plan a route of repentance and returning?

5. If the only fragment of Scripture we possessed was Deuteronomy 4, what are some things we could ascertain about God's character and ways?

6. From Deuteronomy 4, list and comment on five of the blessings Israel would enjoy if they embraced God's Law and abided by it.

   a.

   b.

   c.

d.

e.

:: UNDERSTANDING LEGALISM

Do you think you could tell the difference between a legalist and a devout believer just by observation? Probably not. That's because legalism and true devotion describe a person's heart motives and beliefs, not his behavior. The legalist believes that God's favor must be won and retained by a faultless execution of all God's commandments. The devout believer knows that a loving God has already offered His redeeming grace. The legalist obeys the law to gain God's favor. The devout believer obeys the law to avail himself of God's favor freely offered. The former is trying to earn God's love; the latter is relying on it.

7. God spoke the Ten Commandments in the hearing of all Israel, framing for them the two basic categories that all His subsequent statutes would fit into: (1) laws governing people's relationship with God and (2) laws regulating people's relationship with each other. What are the "human-to-God" commandments? What are the "human-to-human" commandments?

:: CATEGORIZING THE COMMANDMENTS

As we've seen, the Ten Commandments can be divided into two categories. However, the whole body of 613 laws has also been divided into the positive ("thou shalt") and negative ("thou shalt not") commandments. In his explanation of the Old Testament Law, Maimonides, an eminent rabbi of the twelfth century, said there were 365 negative laws, one for every day of the year, and 248 positive laws, one for every bone in the human body, according to ancient reckoning. Thus, sages concluded, God sustains the very life of His children every day according to His Law (see 6:24).

8. According to Deuteronomy 5, how did the Israelites react when they heard God utter the Ten Commandments "at the mountain from the midst of the fire, of the cloud and of the thick gloom, with a great voice" (verse 22)?

Why did God approve of their response?

How might you cultivate a similar heart-level response toward God and His Word?

::THE HEART OF IDOLATRY

When we think of *idolatry*, we may envision people bowing down to a statue made of wood or stone. But that outward act simply makes an idolater's mistaken beliefs about God evident. An idolater chiefly errs in that he believes God to be something other than He is and worships Him accordingly — that is, erroneously.[3] In the ancient world, polytheistic idolatry often developed a dark side, where the gods were believed to demand high prices, even human sacrifice, in return for their uncertain favors (see Deuteronomy 12:29-31).

9. Deuteronomy 12; 15; and 17 provide a sampling of the Law of Moses. Using the chart that follows, consider what laws God established for Israel and what reasons lie behind them.

PASSAGE	WHAT LAWS DID GOD ESTABLISH?	WHAT REASON IS STATED OR IMPLIED FOR WHY THESE LAWS ARE GIVEN?
Deuteronomy 12		
Deuteronomy 15		
Deuteronomy 17		

:: LIBERTY AND LAW

What would life be like without law? Many people think it would mean ultimate freedom, the removal of all restrictions. In some sense, this is true. Life would look kind of like an intense, international soccer match with no rules, no referees, and no boundary between the fervent crowd and the playing field. It wouldn't take long for this kind of unfettered freedom to devolve into an all-out brawl. Just laws don't revoke our liberty; they revoke our license to do what is wrong and preserve our power to do what is right.

A NEW TESTAMENT EXCURSION

Read Mark 12:28-34.

Toward the end of His ministry, Jesus faced an increasingly hostile reaction from the religious and political authorities of His day (the Pharisees and Sadducees). Mark 11 and 12 highlight the growing tension between Jesus and these leaders, as they sought out grounds for defaming or destroying Him. In Mark 12:28, an expert in the Law, a scribe, approached Jesus with a question.

1. Did the scribe's question reflect his genuine personal interest or a subtle attempt to trap Jesus in His teaching?

2. How does Jesus answer the scribe's question?

3. How does Jesus' answer square with the two main categories God introduced in the Ten Commandments? (see question 7.)

4. What effect did Jesus' answer have on the scribe? What effect did it have on the other authorities who had been trying to trap Him?

5. What effect does Jesus' answer have on you? How does it challenge your thinking—or your behavior toward God and your neighbor?

Now read Acts 15:1-29.

The first council of the church was convened to consider whether the Law of Moses should be considered binding on Gentiles who were coming to Christ.

6. Using the chart on the next page, summarize the various responses of the church leadership to this question:

SOME BELIEVERS WHO WERE PHARISEES (VERSE 5)	PETER (VERSES 7–11)	BARNABAS AND PAUL (VERSE 12)	JAMES (VERSES 13–21)	THE UNITED COUNCIL (VERSES 22–29)

REFLECTIONS

Listen. See. Know. Remember. Consider. With these and similar words, Moses admonished the people of Israel to "take care, and keep your soul[s] diligently, lest you forget the things that your eyes have seen, and lest they depart from your heart all the days of your life" (Deuteronomy 4:9, ESV).

1. What dangers await us if we fail to think carefully and constructively about the ways of God and the Word He has revealed?

2. How would you describe the gap between hearing a profound truth and "lay[ing] it to your heart" (4:39, ESV)?

3. What is one key truth you have learned about the character or commands of God that you want to lay to your heart? How might you do so?

People speak quite definitely about a Judeo-Christian value system that pervades Western culture. Think about the laws you studied in Deuteronomy.

4. Did you see any specific laws that have been carried over into our culture today?

5. Did you perceive any overarching values that influence our culture?

6. On the other hand, what sections of the Law seemed largely irrelevant to today?

INTERSECTIONS

Often when people set out to read through the Old Testament, they hit Leviticus, where the Law is expounded, and bog down. "What drudgery!" many people conclude . . . and then they quit. Yet the writers of the Bible considered the Law of Moses anything but boring.

1. Examine 2 Kings 22–23 and Psalm 119, and describe the attitude or reaction of people to the Law of Moses.

Much of the conflict Jesus had with the religious establishment of His day centered around their reliance on "the tradition of the elders" rather than the Scriptures (see, for example, Matthew 15:1-9). This body of teaching, a work in process in Jesus' day, has been handed down to us in the complete collection called the Talmud.

2. Do a bit of investigation into the composition and character of the Talmud using an online encyclopedia (such as www.wikipedia.com). Look especially at an overview of the contents and a sample of its regulations. You might also conduct a simple web search for the tractate (or volume) "Ethics of the Fathers," which is one of the best-known and best-loved works within the Talmud. How would you characterize the Talmud based on your initial look into it?

LAY IT TO YOUR HEART

Meditate on the following passages and commit them to memory:

- Open my eyes, that I may behold wonderful things from Your law. (Psalm 119:18)
- The LORD was pleased for His righteousness' sake to make the law great and glorious. (Isaiah 42:21)
- For this is the love of God, that we keep His commandments; and His commandments are not burdensome. (1 John 5:3)

::6

GOD'S DWELLING AMONG HIS PEOPLE

ACCOMMODATIONS FIT FOR A KING ::

Suppose a foreign dignitary was moving to your town to live for several years. If you were on the committee responsible for arranging accommodations for this official, where would you have him stay? Would any economy hotel do? What about a more permanent apartment or even a house in a neighborhood that corresponded to the person's status?

Or perhaps you might opt for the seventeen-year-old tent camper that has been stored in your neighbor's barn. But then again . . . probably not.

This scenario is much like the situation in Israel until Solomon built a temple for the Lord in Jerusalem. Since Moses' time, the only habitation God had enjoyed among His people was a portable tent. In the days of the Exodus from Egypt and the conquest of Canaan, this richly designed tabernacle was a practical and suitable place of worship.

But times had changed, and Israel was no longer a nation on the move. The Israelites had settled in a rich land and enjoyed a flourishing culture. They were strategically positioned in the Mediterranean world to enjoy commercial relations with Europe, Asia, and Africa. And the great warrior-king David had not only subjugated the surrounding nations but also extended and secured Israel's borders.

Yet amid all this progress and splendor, the God of Israel was still accommodated in a tent. The irreconcilable irony of it all was not lost on David, and the king took it into his heart to build a great house for the Lord (see 2 Samuel 7:1-2). David dedicated a vast amount of his personal wealth and received generous offerings from the people for the construction of the temple. He even received directions for the design of the temple and its fixtures "from the hand of the LORD" (1 Chronicles 28:19, ESV).

Even so, it wasn't David's destiny to build the Lord's temple. That honor belonged to his son Solomon, whose breadth of wisdom and skill in governance ushered Israel from the foothills of national stability to the peak of international renown.

Solomon brought the golden age of Israel to its zenith, such that "Judah and Israel lived in safety, every man under his vine and his fig tree, from Dan even to Beersheba, all the days of Solomon" (1 Kings 4:25). Having brought rest to His people, the Lord decided it was a fitting time for His presence to rest among His people in a glorious house.

But why build such a great God a house at all? Could it be that He actually lived inside it? If not, what did the temple represent? What did it stand for? To answer these questions, look to the book of 1 Kings and delve into the mystery along with the wisest man who ever lived.

THE OPEN ROAD

Read 1 Kings 4:29–9:9.

1. Solomon was renowned all over the Near Eastern world for his wisdom (see 10:23-25). What examples of Solomon's wisdom are given in 1 Kings 4:29–5:18?

::FOUR TEMPLES

The Bible makes reference to four temples in Jerusalem: (1) *Solomon's temple* was the first one to be constructed. (2) The *temple in Ezekiel's vision* was never actually built but gave us divine insight into God's concern for His house. (3) *Zerubbabel's temple* was built after the Jews returned to Jerusalem from exile in Babylon. (4) And *Herod's temple*, the one standing in Jesus' day, was a renovated and greatly expanded version of Zerubbabel's temple. After the Roman general Titus destroyed Herod's temple in AD 70, none has been rebuilt in its place.

2. Solomon left the following insight for all who would follow in his footsteps: "The beginning of wisdom is: Acquire wisdom" (Proverbs 4:7). What sense do you make of this advice?

Describe two personal commitments you have made—or could make—to acquire wisdom.

::WOULDN'T A MAILBOX DO?

Solomon announced as he began constructing the temple, "I intend to build a house for the name of the LORD my God" (1 Kings 5:5). But why would an elaborate building be raised only to house someone's *name*? In the ancient world, a name was not an arbitrary label attached to a baby at birth. Rather, a person's name was synonymous with the person himself. It represented the very essence of the individual it was bestowed upon. To change a person's name was to alter his destiny. To speak in a person's name was to represent his thoughts with his personal authority. To take God's name in vain was to trivialize His dignity and denigrate His sovereignty. Thus, to build a house for His name was to welcome His presence and worship His majesty.

3. Read the details of the temple's structural and interior design with your imagination in full gear, trying to envision what it must have looked like (1 Kings 6). What significant structural elements (materials and dimensions) of the temple stand out to you?

   What observations do you make about its interior design (such as ornamentation and proportions)?

   Why do you suppose Solomon built the temple with such superior materials and intricate detail?

4. How does beauty and splendor relate to your worship of God? Do your surroundings affect your sense of awe when worshiping the Lord?

::THE UGLY TRUTH

"Beauty is not mere ornamentation that we dutifully defer until the coming of the New Jerusalem. It is an essential part of our Gospel, which must be manifest now as we bear witness to kingdom life. . . . If we neglect beauty in our homes, in our churches and in the education of our children, we will be cultivating . . . a deficient religion: the heresy of an unbeautiful Christianity."[1] —John G. Stackhouse

5. According to 1 Kings 8:4, the ark of the covenant of the Lord and the holy vessels from the tabernacle were the final articles to be brought into the new temple. Describe the mood of the people as these things were being transported to the temple.

   Where did the ark finally come to rest within the temple?

   Given the contents of the ark (1 Kings 8:9) and the immediate response of God to its finding rest in the temple (1 Kings 8:10-11), what do you infer about the ark's significance?

::THE LOST ARK

Where is the ark of the covenant today? If we knew the answer, Harrison Ford would never have gotten to star in the *Raiders of the Lost Ark* movies. It is fair to assume that the ark was destroyed when Nebuchadnezzer's army razed Jerusalem and burned Solomon's temple around 587 BC (see 2 Kings 25:8-9). The ark does not figure in the prophecies or narratives about the rebuilding of the second temple. In fact, God promised through Jeremiah that it would not be mentioned, missed, or remade after the restoration from exile (see Jeremiah 3:16).

6. How would you describe the balance of credit Solomon ascribes to his father David, to himself, and to the Lord for the building of the temple in 1 Kings 8:12-21?

7. How can you develop a mindset like Solomon's with regard to your own accomplishments in life? (Compare David's prayer in 1 Chronicles 29:10-19 and the warning Moses offered in Deuteronomy 8:11-18 as you reflect on this.)

8. List some of the circumstances under which Solomon envisioned the Jewish people invoking God's help at the temple, followed by the response Solomon asked of the Lord.

PASSAGE (1 KINGS 8)	UNDER WHAT CIRCUMSTANCES IS GOD'S NAME INVOKED IN OR TOWARD THE TEMPLE?	HOW DOES SOLOMON ASK GOD TO RESPOND?
verses 31-32		
verses 33-34		
verses 35-36		
verses 37-40		
verses 41-43		
verses 44-45		
verses 46-51		

9. What feature(s) do each of the circumstances listed on page 90 share in common? What negative aspects of human nature does Solomon count on? What positive aspects of God's nature does he count on?

:: A BOOTH WITH A VIEW

Solomon chose to dedicate the temple in the seventh month of the year following its completion, when all Israel would have been gathered in Jerusalem to celebrate the Feast of Booths (see Leviticus 23:33-43). During this seven-day convocation, the people of Israel built temporary dwellings to commemorate the forty years they wandered in the wilderness. What a fitting time for the dedication of the temple! All Israel could look out from their makeshift shelters to see that God was no longer worshiped in a tent but in a temple that towered above the capital city.

10. What realities did Solomon recognize in the benediction he spoke to the people of Israel (1 Kings 8:54-61)?

What did Solomon desire of God?

What did Solomon ask of the nation of Israel?

What did he hope for the nations around Israel?

11. After Solomon had built and dedicated the temple, God appeared to him in a vision (1 Kings 9:1-9). What confirmation did God give Solomon about the temple?

What would become of the temple and of Israel if Solomon or his sons (the future kings) rejected God?

:: THE SHEKINAH

Although "no one has ever seen God" (John 1:18, ESV), He revealed Himself to Israel in the form of a cloud of glory, known as the *Shekinah* (from a Hebrew root, meaning "to dwell"). The *Shekinah* led Israel out of Egypt (Exodus 40:34-38); shrouded Mount Sinai when Moses received the Law (Exodus 19:17-18); descended on Solomon's temple (1 Kings 8:10-11); and ultimately departed from the temple before its destruction (Ezekiel 10:18-19). The *Shekinah* did not reappear on earth again until "the Word became flesh and dwelt among us" (John 1:14).

A NEW TESTAMENT EXCURSION

Read Luke 18:9-14.

Jesus told His followers a story of two men who enter the temple in Jerusalem to pray. Compare the prayers these two men offered with the kind of prayers Solomon anticipated coming from God's people in the temple (see question 9 above).

1. How would you characterize the prayer offered by the Pharisee?

   What about the prayer of the tax collector?

2. What lesson did Jesus want His followers to learn from this parable?

Now read Luke 21:5-37.

Jesus' disciples found Herod's temple to be a very impressive structure. As they left Jerusalem one day, they exclaimed to Jesus about its grandeur. Jesus seized the opportunity to startle them into the recognition that the temple era was drawing to a close.

3. What did Jesus predict would happen to the temple in Jerusalem?

4. What question did Jesus' comment provoke from His disciples?

5. As Jesus followed up on His disciples' question, He directed their thoughts beyond the destruction of the Holy City (21:20-24) to the end of days (21:25-36). What kind of lives did Jesus want His followers to live in the midst of such calamities?

REFLECTIONS

The temple was not just a building—it was a sign, a standing reminder of God's authoritative presence among His people and a symbol of their reverence for Him. Though God does not expect every follower of His to build a temple for Him, He does expect us to live with a reverent awareness of His presence.

1. What disciplines of thought and behavior help you to retain such an awareness of God?

2. What daily habits could you foster to acknowledge God's presence, thank Him for His mercy, or ask Him for His guidance?

Solomon poses a provocative question in 1 Kings 8:27: "But will God indeed dwell on the earth?"

3. How is that question answered differently by various religions?

4. How is it answered by modern spiritualists who don't associate with traditional religions?

5. In what respect could a person say that God "resided" in the temples Solomon or Zerubbabel built—or that He did not?

INTERSECTIONS

The temple was not designed merely to be gazed at by awed onlookers in Jerusalem. It was a place where Jews came to worship God. Much of their worship involved bringing animals to the priests to be sacrificed in the temple and burned on the great bronze altar. With so many sacrifices, it is no wonder that a great "sea of cast metal" (1 Kings 7:23), capable of holding more than 2,000 gallons of water, stood in the temple courtyard.

1. Examine Leviticus 1–7 and note on the next page the various sacrifices God prescribed. The reason for each offering may be stated explicitly or implied by the name.

THE OFFERING	WHAT WAS SACRIFICED?	WHY WOULD A PERSON BRING THIS OFFERING?
Burnt offering (Leviticus 1)		
Grain offering (Leviticus 2)		
Peace offerings (Leviticus 3 — the peace offering includes the thanksgiving, vow, and freewill offerings of Leviticus 7.)		
Sin offerings (Leviticus 4:1–5:13)		
Guilt offerings (Leviticus 5:14–6:7)		

Consider the current status of the temple in Jerusalem.

2. On the site where the temple once stood, the Muslim shrine called The Dome of the Rock now stands. Describe the conflict that has centered on this spot historically and offer some reasons the conflict exists currently.

3. What groups are involved in the struggle? What stake does each have in the Temple Mount?

LAY IT TO YOUR HEART

Meditate on the following passages and commit them to memory:

- "But will God indeed dwell on the earth? Behold, heaven and the highest heaven cannot contain You, how much less this house which I have built!" (1 Kings 8:27)
- Thus says the Lord, "Heaven is My throne and the earth is My footstool. Where then is a house you could build for Me? And where is a place that I may rest?" (Isaiah 66:1)

- "And the nations will know that I am the LORD who sanctifies Israel, when My sanctuary is in their midst forever." (Ezekiel 37:28)

::7

A SUFFERING SOVEREIGN

ANTICIPATING THE MESSIAH'S APPEARANCE ::

Ever since sin was introduced by the fall of mankind, human beings have lived with a deep-seated awareness that something is wrong with the world. Alongside this core conviction, we have a sense that someone should come to make it right again. To this universal human longing, the Old Testament presents definite promises about a person who would come to set things right. He is called the Messiah.

So far, our study of biblical themes appearing to the "left of Matthew" has progressed in chronological fashion: Creation precedes the Fall, which precedes God's choice of Abraham, and so forth. As we come to the Messiah, however, we find that revelations about Him are scattered throughout the Old Testament. Prophecies that foretold His coming became clearer in later years, but His appearance was actually predicted as early as the third chapter of Genesis.

When God curses the serpent, He says, "I will put enmity between you and the woman, and between your seed and her seed; He shall bruise you on the head, and you shall bruise him on the heel" (Genesis

3:15). Scarcely could Satan himself have understood this pronouncement as a reference to the Messiah. Yet something in the saying was more portentous than a decree that men would fear snakes.

That is the sort of thing you notice about prophecy in the Old Testament: It was applicable to the people who heard it pronounced, *and* it provided a vista beyond the immediate situation. To put it another way, there's always a primary meaning that the hearers could scarcely miss *and* a fuller meaning—an implication—that the hearers could scarcely imagine.

Old Testament prophets were not commissioned by God to utter generic, fortune-cookie platitudes about what would inevitably happen anyway. Nor did they gaze into crystals and prognosticate the birthdates of celebrities to appear centuries later. They spoke candidly to their immediate listeners about contemporary matters. Yet they also spoke beyond them, seeing in the bright light of the here-and-now a shadow of something to come.

God's curse in Genesis 3:15 clearly indicated or explained the pervasive enmity between humans and snakes. In doing so, though, God opened up a panorama for His people to envision the final destruction of the Evil One. Thus, Isaiah could describe the messianic era as a return to Eden when "the wolf and the lamb will graze together, and the lion will eat straw like the ox; *and dust will be the serpent's food*" (Isaiah 65:25, emphasis added). What's more, Paul could speak of the imminent return of the Messiah as the time when "the God of peace will soon crush Satan under your feet" (Romans 16:20).

Admittedly, this primer on Old Testament prophecy is insufficient to prepare you to encounter all the rich predictions about the Messiah in the Old Testament. But perhaps it will be adequate to train your attention on the Servant whom Isaiah saw (see Isaiah 42).

Jewish commentators who do not accept Jesus as the Messiah are right to insist that Isaiah was speaking about Israel as God's servant. How else is one to interpret passages such as Isaiah 41:8-10 and 42:19, which refer to Israel? Yet it is equally clear that Isaiah was speaking *beyond* Israel even as he was speaking *to* Israel. He pointed to a time in the future when Someone would come to suffer rejection, bring redemption, and assume universal sovereignty over the nations. No one could have invented a character who actually lived out all these predictions, but some did believe Him when He stood in a synagogue, read the messianic prophecy of Isaiah 61, and announced, "Today this Scripture has been fulfilled in your hearing" (Luke 4:21).

THE OPEN ROAD

Read Isaiah 40:1–42:13; 52:1–53:12.

One commentator has described the transition from Isaiah 39 to Isaiah 40 as something like waking up from a hundred-and-fifty-year sleep. Israel's demise, prophesied at the end of Isaiah 39, has finished as chapter 40 opens up on the dawn of God's restoration.

1. According to Isaiah 40:1-12, how is this restoration announced to Israel?

::CHOOSE YOUR TERMS

We derive our English word *Christ* from the Greek term *christos*, which means "the anointed one." *Christos* was the best Greek translation of the underlying Hebrew term for "the anointed one," *mashiach*, from which we derive our English word *Messiah*. In the Old Testament, kings or other rulers were anointed with oil to symbolize that God had divinely selected them to serve as agents of His redemptive purposes.

2. In Isaiah 40:6-8, the eternal nature of God's Word is contrasted with the fleeting nature of human existence. In what ways does this revelation challenge you? How does it comfort you?

:: THE PROPHETIC PAST TENSE

In the Old Testament, many prophecies about the future are expressed in the past tense. Why? To indicate the certainty of the divine plan to bring these things to pass. For a God with the power to call "into being that which does not exist" (Romans 4:17), a prophecy about the future is issued with as much assurance as if it had already happened.

3. How does Isaiah speak of God's greatness in relation to His creation (40:12-31)?

   What effect should this knowledge have on a people who feel that God has forgotten about them?

4. What direction do you find in Isaiah 40:12-31 for remaining steadfast during times of hardship?

   What is the Lord asking you to reflect on if you feel He has deserted you in your troubles?

5. When Isaiah 41 opens, God summons the idol-worshiping adversaries of Israel to consider that He is raising up a mighty conqueror to subdue their nations and kings (see Isaiah 45:1-3; 46:10-11). How do the nations respond to this announcement?

   How does God instruct His people to react to the news?

   What purposes does He have in mind for them?

::A PERSIAN MESSIAH?

In Isaiah 41, God indicated that He would raise up a ruler to vanquish the enemies of Israel. In Isaiah 45:1, the Lord identifies this ruler by his name — Cyrus. A Persian monarch, Cyrus overthrew the kingdom of Babylon in 538 BC and issued an edict permitting the exiled Jews to return home to rebuild the temple in Jerusalem (see Ezra 1:1-4). Because Cyrus played such a central role in bringing about God's redemptive plan for His people, God actually called this Persian monarch "His anointed" — His messiah.

6. In Isaiah 41:21-29, God laid down a challenge—a dare, if you will—to the idol-worshiping nations. What did He ask them to do?

7. Having established the fact that He alone can infallibly forecast the future, God spoke of another Servant—the Messiah—coming to minister to the people. How would you characterize the Messiah's relationship to God as it is presented in Isaiah 42?

   Describe the kind of ministry the Servant will have among God's people. What will be the results of His ministry?

8. According to Isaiah 42:10-13, how far would God's salvation extend through the Messiah?

   What response does His ministry elicit from the people?

   What kind of response do these descriptions of the Messiah's ministry stir up in you?

::THE SON OF DAVID

In both biblical and extrabiblical literature, the Messiah is often designated "the son of David" (Matthew 12:23; 21:9; 22:41-46). God had established an immutable covenant with David assuring him that his descendants would occupy the throne of Israel forever (2 Samuel 7:16). After Solomon's demise and the eventual destruction of the Israelite kingdom, the prophets came to understand that God's promise implied the Messiah to be born in David's line, yet whose unique relation to

God from the beginning of time afforded Him a sovereign rule over Israel and all earthly kingdoms (Psalm 2).

9. As Isaiah continues with his prophecy, he recognizes that a time of severe judgment lies ahead for Israel, with no one to comfort or guide God's people. Even so, the days of restoration are as sure as the days of judgment. How would you describe the tone of God's announcement to Israel in Isaiah 52:1-12?

10. Just as Israel suffered God's judgment through slavery and exile, so the Messiah would also experience God's judgment against sin. The Servant would be one who saves through suffering. How does the prophet speak of the Messiah's disfigurement in Isaiah 52:13–53:12?

    What reaction do people have to the Messiah? What do they presume about His relationship with God?

11. Why did it please God to crush the Messiah (see Isaiah 53:10)? What did the Servant's suffering accomplish for God's people?

::AFTER THE MESSIAH

When would the Messiah come? No prophet knew the answer to this question (see 1 Peter 1:10-12), nor were people encouraged to speculate about His coming . . . or His second coming. Nevertheless, a tradition developed among the Jewish sages that was recorded in the authoritative compendium of oral law and biblical commentary known as the Talmud. There, the sages generally held that "the world will endure six thousand years — two thousand years in chaos, two thousand with Torah, and two thousand years will be the days of the Messiah."[1]

12. In what ways do the two pictures of the Messiah in Isaiah 42 and Isaiah 53 contrast?

How might these contrasting pictures of the same Messiah lead to different expectations of what His ministry would look like when He came?

::ROOM FOR REJECTION

Why did God not foretell the coming of the Messiah in terms more definite than what we find in Old Testament prophecies? Because God chose to hide Himself (see Isaiah 45:15), such that people of faith and goodwill would be responsive to Jesus' teaching while the hard-hearted would turn away. Thus, Jesus said to those Jews who had already rejected Him, "You do not have His word abiding in you, for you do not believe Him whom He sent. You search the Scriptures because you think that in them you have eternal life; it is these that testify about Me; and you are unwilling to come to Me so that you may have life" (John 5:38-40). God left enough room in the messianic prophecies for each person to make a legitimate choice to accept or reject Jesus as the Messiah.

A NEW TESTAMENT EXCURSION

You cannot turn in your Bible to the right of Malachi and continue to speak about the Messiah in an abstract way. From the opening sentence of the New Testament canon, we discover that we are reading "the record of the genealogy of Jesus the Messiah" (Matthew 1:1). The Messiah is not speculative or theoretical notion but a real person. He is not a concept but a carpenter from Galilee. And when people met Him face to face, they inevitably arrived at a crossroads in life.

1. Describe how each of the following people responded to Jesus when they met Him. How were their expectations fulfilled or thwarted? What was the outcome of their encounters?

   The magi or wise men. (Matthew 2:1-11)

   John the Baptist. (Matthew 3:11-17; 11:1-6)

   The scribes and Pharisees. (Matthew 9:1-13)

   The people of Nazareth. (Matthew 13:53-58)

REFLECTIONS

News flash: The Messiah has come—and He wasn't you. In God's wisdom, you were not given the responsibility to secure forgiveness for yourself or establish justice for the nations. You actually weren't even asked to make yourself responsible for a single day! This is great news, even if self-reliant people sometimes find it hard to swallow.

1. Describe some scenarios in your life where you are prone to develop a "Messiah complex" and begin to think you must save yourself or others from troubles. What burden does this place on your shoulders?

2. How do the teachings from Isaiah remind you of the truth and relieve you of such pressure?

A lot of people today respect Jesus as a "good teacher" but reject Him as the Son of God. In many ways, this is an advantage when sharing the gospel, since a person who respects Jesus as a teacher will presumably be more inclined to listen to His teachings. Even so, the Messiah's ministry is not characterized in Isaiah as a ministry of teaching or preaching or moralizing to the masses.

3. What passages from Isaiah could you turn to with a friend to say, "This is what the ministry of the Messiah was supposed to accomplish"?

4. What passages from the New Testament affirm that Jesus' ministry aligned with Isaiah's prophecies?

INTERSECTIONS

The ministry and identity of the Messiah do not hang on one isolated text in Isaiah. Multiple passages by many authors throughout the Old Testament speak of the coming Savior.

1. Examine the sampling of passages that follows and consider what each tells us about the advent, mission, or identity of the Messiah.

PASSAGE	WHAT DO YOU DISCOVER ABOUT THE ADVENT, MISSION, OR IDENTITY OF THE MESSIAH?
Deuteronomy 18:15-19	
Isaiah 9:2-7	
Micah 5:2-4	
Malachi 3:1-4	

2. As you consider the passages from the chart above along with Isaiah 42:1-9, think through the open doors for ministry you have to the people around you. Who are the three main people (or groups of people) you rub shoulders with during an average week? No doubt, these are some of the very people God wants to reach through you. Offer some concrete ideas about how the stated direction of the Messiah's mission on earth could lend direction to your ministry among these people.

LAY IT TO YOUR HEART

Meditate on the following passages and commit them to memory:

- "I see him, but not now; I behold him, but not near; a star shall come forth from Jacob, a scepter shall rise from Israel." (Numbers 24:17)
- But He was pierced through for our transgressions, He was crushed for our iniquities; the chastening for our well-being fell upon Him, and by His scourging we are healed. (Isaiah 53:5)
- Afterward the sons of Israel will return and seek the LORD their God and David their king; and they will come trembling to the LORD and to His goodness in the last days. (Hosea 3:5)

:: 8

ANTICIPATING THE DAWN

THE PROMISE OF A NEW COVENANT AND A NEW ERA ::

In history, Jeremiah is known as "the weeping prophet" because of the intense grief he felt over Israel's imminent doom. In his own day, he was reviled as a pessimist, rejected as a prophet, and imprisoned as an adversary of the government. He lived through the eighteen-year overthrow of Judah and died among faithless cowards who fled the kingdom to meet an ignominious end in Egypt.

In short, no prophet in the Old Testament ever spoke as much truth as Jeremiah and suffered as much for it. We should all be glad to *read* his story rather than to *live* it.

Yet somehow, as Jeremiah endured many dark days, he saw a great light on the horizon. Not only did he perceive the coming Messiah—"a righteous Branch of David to spring forth" (Jeremiah 33:15)—he also saw that God was preparing to change the terms by which He related to man. The Lord was preparing to establish a new covenant with His people.

Throughout their history, Abraham's descendants had believed that the entire universe was ruled by one God who related to people solely and consistently on the basis of covenants He revealed to them. In this regard, the Jews stood apart from all other ancient civilizations. The rest of the nations in the ancient world believed in a pantheon of gods, devils, and spirits, whose behavior toward humans was about as predictable as a tornado. Those ancient people didn't so much worship their gods as try to curry their favor or avoid their wrath.

The God of Abraham was not like that. He stood alone as the Sovereign of the universe, yet He related to His people with consistent grace on the basis of revealed covenants.

You've already learned about some of God's covenants: God established a covenant with Noah after the flood; He established a covenant with Abraham in Haran; and He established a long-standing covenant with the nation of Israel at Sinai when He gave them the Law. In fact, Israel had lived under the covenant of the Law for so long—more than a millennium—that a person could scarcely imagine life without it.

That is why it is so striking that the weeping prophet, the one no one liked or listened to, gazed out of his prison cell across the horizon of history and saw the dawn of a new era. We may be thankful that God's revelation to Jeremiah began, "Write all the words which I have spoken to you in a book" (30:2). What he wrote is available for us to read, and there is good reason to read it with care. After all, we are now living under the New Covenant!

THE OPEN ROAD

Read Jeremiah 30-33.

::THE EXILE FROM EVERY ANGLE

While Jeremiah was the only prophet to live through the destruction of Jerusalem, the Bible provides us with two other eyewitnesses to this period of history. Daniel was one of the young noblemen taken to Babylon from Jerusalem around 605 BC. He provides insight into the Babylonian and Persian kingdoms of the time. Ezekiel, a priest and prophet, was swept away in a second wave of deportation in 597 BC and offers a closer look at the Jewish community in exile. Jeremiah lived through the final destruction of Judah in 586 BC and witnessed the faithless flight to Egypt of the remnant of people who were left behind.

Jeremiah 30 bounces back and forth between descriptions of Israel's present calamity under God's judgment and promises about the nation's restoration. The chapter ends with this compelling, if cryptic, statement: "In the latter days you will understand this." One key to understanding the double-vision of this chapter is to distinguish between present-tense and future-tense verbs.

1. By noting the shifts in verb tenses, jot down some differences regarding Israel's present condition and its future hopes in Jeremiah 30:

ISRAEL'S PRESENT CONDITION UNDER GOD'S JUDGMENT	ISRAEL'S FUTURE HOPES AFTER GOD'S RESTORATION

2. What good things did the Lord make Himself responsible for in Jeremiah 31:1-14?

3. Describe Israel's response to God's restoration?

4. How does your belief about God's character (His sovereignty, integrity, goodwill, and so on) influence your response to these promises?

:: DAVID REINCARNATE?

Jeremiah foresaw that Israel would someday be restored to serve "the LORD their God and David their king, whom I [the Lord] will raise up for them" (30:9). Was Jeremiah teaching a foreign doctrine of reincarnation? No. As it turns out, by Jeremiah's day, the name "David" had become synonymous with "the coming Messiah." When the Aramaic-speaking Jews of the first century BC translated the Hebrew Scriptures, they removed all doubt by rendering this passage, "Messiah, Son of David their king."

5. Jeremiah identifies a proverb current among the exiles from Judah: "The fathers have eaten sour grapes, and the children's teeth are set on edge" (31:29). What do you think this saying means?

6. Jeremiah insisted that this proverb would no longer be repeated in the time of the New Covenant: "In those days they will not say again, 'The fathers have eaten sour grapes, and the children's teeth are set on edge'" (31:29). Why do you think this is so?

::RIGHT OF MALACHI

Being familiar with the division of the Bible into the Old and New Testaments, you already know more than you may realize about the New Covenant. The English word *testament* is a translation (via Latin) of the Hebrew word for *covenant*. Every time you turn the pages in your Bible from Malachi to Matthew, you are tacitly acknowledging the distinction between the Old and New Covenants.

7. Jeremiah 31:31-40 offers the most explicit teaching in all of Scripture about the New Covenant. With whom does God promise to make this covenant?

8. What is the status of the former covenant—the Mosaic Law—God made with Israel when He led them out of Egypt (see Ezekiel 16:59-60)?

What are the key differences between the New Covenant and the former one?

How will God deal with people's sins under the New Covenant?

:: DON'T MISS THIS MESSAGE

Biblical commentator Charles Feinberg says of Jeremiah 31:31-40, "It has been acclaimed as one of the most important passages in the entire Old Testament. . . . Many expositors maintain that the concept of the new covenant is Jeremiah's greatest contribution to biblical truth."[1]

9. The opening verses of Jeremiah 32 pull us back from the distant horizon of future restoration to Jeremiah's present plight in a city under siege. What lessons did the Lord intend to teach Jeremiah when He commanded him to buy his cousin's field?

Some of our grandparents may have described a person's commitment to a radical course of action as "selling the farm." You could reverse that metaphor to describe Jeremiah's demonstration of faith in chapter 32: He bought the farm! He didn't merely hear God's promises about restoration and profess a belief in them; he trusted God enough to act on what God promised.

10. In what areas of your life have you found it most difficult to "buy the farm"—to trust God enough to stake your practical decisions on His promises?

:: A SPIRITED FAMILY

The last great king to rule in Judah was a man named Josiah. Josiah's heart was inclined toward the Lord from his earliest days, but his reforms in Judah were expanded significantly when he discovered a hidden copy of the Book of the Law in the temple at Jerusalem. To confirm that he was holding an actual written version of the covenant God had made with Israel, Josiah consulted a straight-shooting prophetess who lived in the capital city. Her name was Huldah (see 2 Chronicles 34:22). Huldah had a nephew by the name of Jeremiah (see Jeremiah 32:7).

11. Consider Jeremiah's prayer in 32:16-25 and fill in the chart below. Note why each character trait ascribed to God was significant in Jeremiah's day and why it is significant in your life.

GOD IS . . .	SIGNIFICANCE IN JEREMIAH'S DAY	SIGNIFICANCE IN MY LIFE
The Sovereign Creator, for whom nothing is difficult (Jeremiah 32:17).	*Jeremiah had to trust that God could preserve the Jewish people in exile and would later bring them back to their homeland.*	*With my finances low, I know I need to trust God to get me through the coming months. He can do anything.*

12. According to Jeremiah 32:26-44, why had God resolved to destroy Jerusalem?

In days to come, how will God change the people's fortunes?

How will He change their hearts?

13. In Jeremiah 33:1-13, how is the condition of Jerusalem and its people living under God's judgment contrasted with Jeremiah's prophecy of Jerusalem and its people living under the New Covenant?

JERUSALEM AND ITS PEOPLE LIVING UNDER GOD'S JUDGMENT	JERUSALEM AND ITS PEOPLE LIVING UNDER THE NEW COVENANT

14. In what ways does (or doesn't) the description of life under the New Covenant reflect the reality of your life with God?

15. In the latter half of Jeremiah 33, what additional promises did the Lord vow to fulfill during the era of the New Covenant? (Feel free to cross-check Genesis 8:22; Numbers 18:21-24; and 2 Samuel 7:16 for the covenants God made with the day and night, the Levites, and David, respectively.)

A NEW TESTAMENT EXCURSION

Read Matthew 26:26-29.

In chapter 4 of this study, you reflected on the significance of the Last Supper (a Passover *seder*) in relation to the biblical idea of deliverance.

1. How do Jesus' words during the Passover meal shed additional light on your understanding of the New Covenant?

Now read Hebrews 8:1-13.

In this passage, the writer of Hebrews draws our attention to a *better ministry* than that of the Old Testament priests carried out under a *better covenant* than the Mosaic Law and enacted on *better promises.*

2. How is the priestly ministry of Jesus a better ministry than the one carried on by the Jewish priests, who served in the tent and temple?

3. According to verse 6, what role does Jesus play in the New Covenant?

4. Why was the former regulation—the first covenant or Mosaic Law—set aside?

5. According to verse 13, what is the current status of the Mosaic Law?

REFLECTIONS

In the four chapters of Jeremiah that you have studied (30-33), God makes more than seventy promises of blessing to His children living under the New Covenant. (You can count them by highlighting every expression that begins "I will. . . .")

1. What if you genuinely took God up on just one of these promises, orienting your thinking and living around His commitments to you? Which promise from Jeremiah 30–33 would you choose?

2. How could you consistently and thoughtfully lay this promise to your heart?

3. How should you respond if the fleeting experiences of a day or a month or even a decade make it seem unlikely that you will see this promise realized?

4. What would be the cumulative effect on your life if you decided to take God up on all of His seventy-plus promises from these chapters?

Many people today believe that all religions teach fundamentally the same truths about faith and lead their adherents to a common eternal end.

5. How is this belief (called "universalism") challenged by the biblical doctrine that God makes and keeps specific covenants with humanity?

6. Consider whether the Mosaic Law and the New Covenant teach fundamentally the same truths. In what ways do the scope, duration, and terms of these two covenants differ?

INTERSECTIONS

As you might suspect, Jeremiah was not the only prophet to foretell something so radical as a sweeping new agreement between God and His people. He was joined by the likes of Isaiah and Ezekiel, who looked toward the restoration of Israel from exile and the coming of the Messiah. They saw this as a crossroads where God would enter into a new kind of relationship with Israel and the Gentile nations. (You might remember from your readings in Isaiah that the Messiah Himself would be the crux of the covenant between God and His people. See, for example, Isaiah 42:6.)

1. What further light do the following prophecies shed on your knowledge of the New Covenant?

   Isaiah 49:5-13

   Isaiah 59:20–60:3

   Ezekiel 36:22-38

Ezekiel 37:24-28

Jesus inaugurated the New Covenant at the Last Supper. However, during His years of ministry, He often signaled that a change in the divine administration was on the way.

2. What do the following passages suggest about Jesus' relation to the Mosaic Law, the standing covenant of His day?

   Matthew 5:17-20

   Matthew 12:1-12

   Matthew 19:1-9,16-21

LAY IT TO YOUR HEART

Meditate on the following passages and commit them to memory:

- "Behold, the former things have come to pass, now I declare new things." (Isaiah 42:9)
- "But this is the covenant which I will make with the house of Israel after those days," declares the LORD, "I will put My law within them and on their heart I will write it; and I will be their God, and they shall be My people." (Jeremiah 31:33)
- "I will give you a new heart and put a new spirit within you; and I will remove the heart of stone from your flesh and give you a heart of flesh." (Ezekiel 36:26)

::9

JUDGMENT JUST OVER THE HORIZON

ALL THINGS MUST COME TO AN END – EVENTUALLY ::

If you'd like to celebrate your arrival at the last chapter of this study guide, maybe you could paint a huge placard that reads, "The End Is Near." It would be fitting in more ways than one.

The end is near. Prophets have been proclaiming this to the friends and enemies of God for hundreds of generations. So long, in fact, that some have begun to wonder whether the end will come at all. Some even scoff at the idea of a final judgment (see 2 Peter 3:3). What these skeptics lack, however, is an adequate appreciation of history. When you read the Old Testament prophets, you discover that God has already brought at least two (if not many more) days of reckoning on His people, events that foreshadow a great and final "Day of the Lord" that will be visited on the whole world.

This is precisely the subject of Joel's prophecy: a three-part vision of God's judgment that *had come* on Israel, that *would come* on Israel again, and that eventually would come against *the whole world*. We know next to nothing about the prophet Joel, the son of Pethuel (Joel 1:1). He left us almost no information about his identity or whereabouts. From the text, we can surmise that he lived during a time of relative prosperity in Israel or Judah prior to the calamitous days of the exile. Several scholars hold that Joel prophesied to the southern kingdom of Judah in the eighth century BC, just before the northern kingdom of Israel was defeated and exiled by the Assyrians.

Although Joel withheld many details about himself, he *did* disclose in three short chapters as much as any prophet could regarding what's to come in the future. Joel saw, through a natural disaster in his own day, the punishing judgment that awaits all who reject God and the purifying judgment God will bring to save the righteous on the Day of the Lord. By the time Joel came onto the scene, many people in Israel had reduced their understanding of the Day of the Lord to mean something like "the time when all Gentiles will meet a well-deserved and untimely demise for opposing the Jews, while all the Jews will be rewarded by God for, well, being Jewish." To correct this mistaken belief with divine revelation, God sent a locust plague against His people—and then a prophet to interpret why it was sent.

Joel saw through the contemporary calamity to two distinct events on history's horizon, each a vision of God setting society right by severe judgment. On the first Day of the Lord, God would deal only with Israel (this happened during the time of the exile). On the final Day of the Lord, God will extend His judgment to the whole world, redeeming the righteous and judging the wicked.

THE OPEN ROAD

Read Joel 1–3.

In Joel 1, we read about Joel's first "vision." Not a mystical experience, this was a calamity every Israelite could see by looking out his window.

1. Describe the physical desolation that Joel saw as he looked around his homeland.

2. Which groups of people felt the effects of the locust plague most grievously?

3. What was the impact of the plague on worship at the house of God?

4. What could possibly be the value of passing down news of this devastation to future generations (Joel 1:3)?

::AN ARMY TEN BILLION STRONG

Scholar G. L. Keown offers this observation: "Once a locust plague begins, it is virtually impossible to control or stop, bringing tremendous destruction to affected areas. Swarms of ten billion locusts periodically enter areas in Africa, southwest Asia, and southern Europe. Areas up to 1,000 square kilometers (400 square miles) can be covered by locust swarms, which leave a barren, denuded landscape in their wake."[1]

5. In Joel 1:13-14, the prophet tried to guide the people's response to this natural disaster by advocating a spiritual return to God. Contrast the kind of return that Joel advocates with two other predictable responses people might have to a locust plague.

6. Joel redirects the attention of his listeners from the things that are happening *around* them to things that are happening *within* them. How do Joel's words provide you direction for coming before God in confession, repentance, and/or trust during times of hardship?

:: A SIMPLE – THOUGH INCORRECT – EXPLANATION

Is all hardship the result of personal sin? No. The equation is not that simple, and Jesus explicitly rejects it in John 9:2-3: "His disciples asked Him, 'Rabbi, who sinned, this man or his parents, that he would be born blind?' Jesus answered, 'It was neither that this man sinned, nor his parents; but it was so that the works of God might be displayed in him.'" (Also see Luke 13:1-5.) Nevertheless, all hardship is a divine invitation to reflect on the state of your soul, repent of any sin, and entrust yourself anew to the sovereign purposes of God.

7. When we come to Joel 1:15, we run into the first reference by Joel to "the day of the LORD." Had that day passed, or was it yet to be?

   How does Joel characterize the Day of the Lord?

Joel 2 records the prophet's second vision. The first verse opens up with a trumpet blast warning Zion that the Day of the Lord is imminent and an invading army is marching toward Israel.

8. What similarities do you observe between the invasion of locusts described in Joel 1 and the invasion of the "great and mighty people" prophesied in Joel 2?

9. Who is leading the northern army against Israel?

How will Israel fare in the face of this second invasion?

10. Compare the descriptions of the Day of the Lord in Joel 2:1-2 and 2:10-11 with the one given in Joel 1:15.

::A KOSHER JUGGERNAUT

Though locusts were considered a kosher food for Jews (see Leviticus 11:20-23), they were also considered a nasty agent of divine judgment. Most notably, God sent "such a dense swarm of locusts" against the land of Egypt that the Pharoah himself publicly confessed his sins to Moses (Exodus 10:14, ESV). John, who recorded Revelation, also foretold a kind of scorpion-like locust horde that will ravage the earth during the Last Days: "In those days men will seek death and will not find it; they will long to die, and death flees from them" (9:6).

11. If you carefully observe the prophet's words in Joel 2, you will discover that the message is not simply one of inevitable judgment but also of potential redemption. What does the second trumpet blast in Joel 2 summon the people to do?

12. Although Joel does not promise that Israel can altogether escape the second Day of the Lord (see Joel 2:20,25), he offers hope if Israel will repent. Characterize the heart attitude with which Israel should turn back to God.

    What sort of reception should Israel expect from God when they turn to Him in repentance?

13. Bible commentator Matthew Henry called the locust plague and the northern army of Joel an "awakening judgment" of God, sent not merely to punish wrongdoers but also to turn them back to God. Have you ever passed through severe trials that helped awaken you to your need for mercy and grace?

14. From Joel 2:28 to the end of the book, we are presented with the prophet's third vision—a vision of the last days. The scope of this prophecy touches on personal relationships with God, international relations with Israel, and cosmic manifestations in the natural realm as the final Day of the Lord draws near. Summarize what Joel has to say about the following:

AS THE FINAL DAY OF THE LORD DRAWS NEAR . . .		
Personal relationships to God (Joel 2:28-29,32)	Cosmic manifestations in the heavens (Joel 2:30-31)	International relations with Israel (Joel 3:1-8)

15. Joel promised that "before the great and awesome day of the LORD comes . . . whoever calls on the name of the LORD will be delivered" (2:31-32). What does it mean for someone to call on the name of the Lord?

Describe the attitude of your heart when you have called on His name.

::REVELATION AND RELATIONSHIP

Like other prophets, Joel saw future events less like a timeline and more like a loose association of symbolically related happenings. Why didn't God spell out the future with more chronologically precise prophecies? It seems that He wanted to leave room in the human experience for wisdom, repentance, and faith. He beckons us to seek Him, rather than benumbing us with facts we can't refute. He tells us enough to inspire our confidence, yet leaves us longing for more divine insight. He rouses us into relationship with Him.

16. According to Joel 3:1-8, why does God bring judgment against the nations?

    How do the nations fare when they muster their warriors to meet the Lord in the valley of decision on the Day of Final Judgment? (3:9-21)

17. Describe the aftereffects of the Day of the Lord for His people. (3:16-21)

A NEW TESTAMENT EXCURSION

Read Acts 2:1-36. You may recall from your past studies of the Messiah and the New Covenant that Jesus celebrated Passover with His disciples just before He was crucified and rose again. Seven weeks after Passover, devout Jews would gather again in Jerusalem to celebrate Pentecost, a holiday commemorating the day when God descended on Mount Sinai and gave His Law to Israel. The events recorded in Acts 2:1-4 speak of a second time God descended on His people at Pentecost.

1. What effects do the "devout men from every nation" (Acts 2:5) observe in the Christians who are filled with the Holy Spirit on Pentecost (Acts 2:6-13)?

2. How does Peter explain to the crowd what they are observing?

3. How does the crowd respond (Acts 2:14-21,37)?

Now read 1 Thessalonians 5:1-11.

From the amount of ink Paul expended to discuss the Day of the Lord, it would appear the Thessalonians were very interested in—and perhaps puzzled about—the topic.

4. How does Paul characterize the Day of the Lord in this passage?

5. How does he encourage Christians to live in light of the Day of the Lord?

6. What destiny will Christians meet with on that day?

REFLECTIONS

Moses offered an excellent principle for ordering our lives when he said, "Teach us to number our days that we may get a heart of wisdom" (Psalm 90:12, ESV). We cannot live wisely through this day if we do not keep the end of days in view. Thomas á Kempis put it this way: "Didst thou oftener think of thy death than of thy living long, there is no question but thou wouldst be more zealous to improve."[2]

1. How might a conscious focus on the Day of the Lord help you to order this life more profitably?

2. How do Joel, Peter (Acts 2), and Paul (1 Thessalonians 5) urge believers to live in light of that day?

3. Can you think of situations in life when it would be foolish or perilous to embark on a journey without a clear notion of your final destination? (Such a personal parable might help anchor this principle in your mind or provide you the means to communicate it with a friend.)

The Day of the Lord is a time of salvation for those who have trusted in Him—and a day of judgment for those who have rejected Him.

4. How could the prospect of divine judgment influence the way a nonbeliever thinks about this life in light of eternity?

5. What beliefs lead some nonbelievers to spurn the threat of divine judgment?

6. What diversions and distractions in this life keep a nonbeliever from thinking about eternity at all?

7. How could you be instrumental in prompting a nonbelieving friend to consider the realities of divine judgment and eternal life?

INTERSECTIONS

During the days of the prophets, many Jews were falsely assured that all Israel would be saved and all Gentiles destroyed on the Day of the Lord. Joel was not the only prophet to dispel this mistaken belief. Read Amos 5:11-20 and Zephaniah 1:1-18, and consider:

1. In what ways is the Day of the Lord characterized?

2. Who will experience judgment on the Day of the Lord?

3. How does the Lord want people to respond in light of these prophecies?

Choose one recent media production (a song, movie, work of art) that attempts to portray the climax—or nadir—of the present age.

4. What parallels, if any, do you observe between this creative composition and the biblical portrait of the Final Judgment?

5. How might your thinking about this modern portrayal provide an open door to talk with nonbelieving friends about the biblical idea of the end of time?

LAY IT TO YOUR HEART

Meditate on the following passages and commit them to memory:

- Alas, you who are longing for the day of the LORD, for what purpose will the day of the LORD be to you? It will be darkness and not light. (Amos 5:18)
- Our Lord Jesus Christ . . . will sustain you to the end, guiltless in the day of our Lord Jesus Christ. (1 Corinthians 1:7-8, ESV)
- Since all these things are to be destroyed in this way, what sort of people ought you to be in holy conduct and godliness, looking for and hastening the coming of the day of God, because of which the heavens will be destroyed by burning, and the elements will melt with intense heat! (2 Peter 3:11-12)

NOTES

CHAPTER ONE: OUR PLACE IN SPACE

1. G. K. Chesterton, *The Everlasting Man* (San Francisco: Ignatius Press, 1993), 17.
2. Mortimer Adler, ed., *The Great Books of the Western World: Pascal*, vol. 33, *Pensées*, II, 72 (Chicago: University of Chicago Press, 1956), 181.
3. Citation of Sanhedrin 4:5 taken from Jacob Neusner, *The Mishnah: A New Translation* (New Haven, CT: Yale University Press, 1988), 591.
4. Mortimer Adler, ed., *The Great Books of the Western World: Lucretius*, vol. 12, *On the Nature of Things*, III, 288 (Chicago: University of Chicago, 1956), 34.
5. Adler, 34.
6. Mortimer Adler, ed., *The Great Books of the Western World: Ptolemy, Copernicus, Kepler*, vol. 16, *The Almagest*, Book I, 6 (Chicago: University of Chicago Press, 1956), 10.

7. See the chapter titled "Job: Seeing in the Dark" in Philip Yancy, *The Bible Jesus Read* (Grand Rapids, MI: Zondervan, 1999), 45-72.
8. Chesterton, 27.

CHAPTER TWO: THE GRAVITY OF OUR FALL

1. Mortimer Adler, ed., *The Great Books of the Western World: Pascal*, vol. 33, *Pensées*, II, 72 (Chicago: University of Chicago Press, 1956), 249.
2. Aleksandr Solzhenitsyn, *The Gulag Archipelago* (New York: Harper & Row, 1973), 168.

CHAPTER THREE: ONE FAMILY FOR ALL NATIONS

1. "Abram" is actually the name used until God changes it to "Abraham" in Genesis 17; however, history has generally erased this distinction, so we will refer to him as "Abraham" throughout this study.
2. Commentary to Genesis 12:6 in Rabbi Nosson Scherman, ed., *The Chumash, The Artscroll Series* / Stone Edition (Brooklyn, NY: Mesorah Publications, 2000), 56.

CHAPTER FIVE: RIGHTEOUSNESS MADE PLAIN

1. Introductory commentary to Deuteronomy, Rabbi Nosson Scherman, ed., *The Chumash, The Artscroll Series* / Stone Edition (Brooklyn, NY: Mesorah Publications, 2000), 938.
2. Philip Yancey, *The Bible Jesus Read* (Grand Rapids, MI: Zondervan, 1999), 93.
3. A. W. Tozer, *The Knowledge of the Holy* (New York: HarperCollins, 1967), 1-5.

CHAPTER SIX: GOD'S DWELLING AMONG HIS PEOPLE

1. John G. Stackhouse, "The True, the Good, and the Beautiful Christian," *Christianity Today* (January 7, 2002), 58.

CHAPTER SEVEN: A SUFFERING SOVEREIGN

1. Cited in Abraham Cohen, *Everyman's Talmud: The Major Teachings of the Rabbinic Sages* (New York: Schocken Books, 1995), 356.

CHAPTER EIGHT: ANTICIPATING THE DAWN

1. Charles Feinberg, commentary on Jeremiah 31:31-34. Cited in Frank E. Gaebelein, ed., *The Expositor's Bible Commentary*, vol. 6 (Grand Rapids, Mich.: Zondervan, 1986), 574.

CHAPTER NINE: JUDGMENT JUST OVER THE HORIZON

1. G. L. Keown, entry on "Locusts." Cited in Geoffrey W. Bromiley, ed., *The International Standard Bible Encyclopedia* (Grand Rapids, Mich.: Eerdmans, 1986), 149-150.
2. Thomas á Kempis, *The Imitation of Christ* (Chicago: Moody, 1984), 67.

ABOUT THE AUTHOR

Norman Hubbard, a native of South Carolina, serves as the campus director for The Navigators at the University of Illinois at Urbana-Campaign. He graduated from Auburn University with an MA in English (applied linguistics). Norman and his wife, Katie, have three children in elementary school.

DIG INTO GOD'S WORD WITH THESE GREAT BIBLE STUDIES.

Right of Malachi

Norman Hubbard

978-1-60006-053-3 1-60006-053-6

This companion study to *Left of Matthew* explores the unifying stories and themes woven throughout Scripture, encouraging readers to actively engage the text and move beyond simple summaries.

Living the Questions in Matthew

The Navigators

978-1-57683-833-4 1-57683-833-1

Many believers think of Jesus as the man with all the answers, sent down to earth to tell us everything we need to know. So why are we still left with so many nagging questions we never seem to find answers for? This study of the gospel of Matthew, using *The Message*—the eye-opening translation by Eugene Peterson—will help you embrace life's questions and build a stronger faith.

Living the Questions in Luke

The Navigators

978-1-57683-861-7 1-57683-861-7

This thought-provoking study of the gospel of Luke will help readers wrestle personally with the often-unsettling questions Jesus asked. Includes text from *The Message*, along with real-life anecdotes and excerpts from literature, pop culture, and current events.

To order copies, visit your local Christian bookstore,
call NavPress at 1-800-366-7788, or log on to www.navpress.com.
To locate a Christian bookstore near you, call 1-800-991-7747.